HUGGING STRANGERS

HUGGING STRANGERS

The Frequent Lows and Occasional Highs
of Football Fandom

JON BERRY

First published by Pitch Publishing, 2020

Pitch Publishing
A2 Yeoman Gate
Yeoman Way
Worthing
Sussex
BN13 3QZ
www.pitchpublishing.co.uk
info@pitchpublishing.co.uk

A CIP catalogue record is available for this book
from the British Library.

. ISBN 978-1-78531-665-4

Typesetting and origination by Pitch Publishing

Printed and bound by TJ International, Padstow, UK

Contents

For the core travelling group: JK, Hextall and his hunches, Kazza and Jimmy the Student. Have fun with stats, Mr K; I think they're all accurate!

In memory of Lou and Horace. One for trying to save me and the other for all he did for my mother.

For Joe, naturally.

Yes, of course you, Babs.

Foreword and disclaimer

I WAS putting the finishing touches to this book in February 2020. After a reasonably promising start to the 2019/20 season, Birmingham City began their traditional slide down the table at around Christmas. I can't count the number of people, most of them reasonably knowledgeable about the game, who dismissed the notion of us being possible relegation candidates as fanciful. It was no use telling them that nearly 57 years of institutional failure had made any such confidence on my part unthinkable.

And then, just to add to the mix, a new dimension has found its way into flirtation with disaster: the points deduction. Having been docked nine points in the 2018/19 season, it was reasonable, even for time-hardened stoics like myself, to think that'd be it for a while. But no. At the time of writing, it seems as though yet more rules may have been broken resulting in more snatching away of hard-earned successes.

With this in mind, there is the possibility that relegation number ten on my watch will have taken place by the time you read this. If, by any absurd chance, we have put together the sort of miracle run that would be needed to propel us into the play-offs, I hereby pledge all royalties for this book to any charity nominated by one of my Villa-supporting mates.

Hugging strangers. Perfectly proper behaviour

IT IS 1.57pm on 7 May 2017. The final whistle blows at Ashton Gate, the home of Bristol City. It is the last game of the season. My team, Birmingham City, has endured an absolute battering for the last 15 minutes, including six minutes of added time. But we have won 1-0 and so have clung on to secure our survival in the second tier of English football. People dance, jiggle around, laugh and cry. I turn to the person next to me and we spontaneously embrace. I don't know him; I am 64 and he looks about 17. It matters not one jot. We slap each other's backs a couple of times and then, entirely unselfconsciously, separate from our momentary clinch. Football lets you do that.

This is a book about being a football supporter. It's true that it's about being a Birmingham City football supporter, but if you're a football supporter, you'll recognise everything that's in here. If you're a football supporter of one of the super-duper elite clubs that wins things on a regular basis, you may find yourself a bit baffled, but I know that there will be honourable exceptions to this. If you watch your football exclusively on the telly or via a computer game, you might struggle a little, but I think you'll get the point.

If you go to football grounds on a regular basis and have supported the same team all your life, you'll be in tune with this book from the start. That'll be even more so if your team is located near to where you were born, currently live or is one with which you have a strong family connection.

It's not a sentimental book and, as you'll see from the early chapters, it does not invoke with nostalgia the crumbling, unsafe and unsanitary stadia that we have left behind. Neither does it advocate clogging people with boots with nailed-in studs (although there's a bit of me that's OK with some of that), nor the removal of all players who take to the pitch in Alice bands and/or gloves, although there's a little bit ...

Because you'll want to know if and when your team features, there's an index that deals with this exclusively. Being a football supporter, I've allowed myself to indulge in a good many of the usual unfounded prejudices that dog our lives, but none of this is too scurrilous. As far as the Villa are concerned, I've been as fair as I can and I've acknowledged, through gritted keyboard, your achievements of the early 1980s.

It's not an attempt at a full historical record and I readily admit that the choices I have made in terms of games and incidents is purely selfish. The accumulation of these personal recollections should furnish you with a pretty full picture of life as a Blues fan. As far as possible, I've avoided blow-by-blow accounts of games other than where these are worth talking about in detail. In many cases, I have relied on the fact that if your interest has been piqued by a match or an incident, you can now find video footage of this online. If you're a Birmingham fan, I may well have missed your favourite game or incident or have failed to mention your favourite player, and you are fully entitled to think that these will be unforgiveable omissions. I offer my apologies in advance, but my contact details appear at the end of the book and you can write to me to tell me why I have been so foolish to have left this out.

As it's a book written in the digital age, I haven't filled its pages with stats, tables and records. These are all readily available. The only full set of results appears right at the start of chapter 1 – and it's worth reading, believe me.

I don't make any claims that there is anything unique about Birmingham City, its history and its supporters. As with most clubs, our story echoes the famous theatre review: great moments, dreadful half hours. 'This could only happen at our club' is the moan in every stand and on every fans' forum. I'm relying on this universality of experience to appeal beyond one team and to all of us who stupidly allow the actions of people we don't know – and who we probably wouldn't like if we met them – to carry our loyalty and affiliation, and with whom we permit our name to be associated.

Birmingham City's wonderful anthem 'Keep Right On' warns us that as we go through life there will be 'joys and sorrows too'. It was probably a matter of getting the scansion and rhythm right in Sir Harry Lauder's poignant song – it was written in memory of his son killed in action in World War One – but the order is, of course, wrong. It should have given precedence to sorrows over joys, although, goodness knows, it's a bit rich to compare this with Lauder's loss. Loyal support means putting up with some dire old garbage in the enduring hope that we'll have great moments, on and off the field of play. And we do – and that's why I wrote this book.

Chapter 1

I am not saved and I savour the smell of football

ON BOXING Day 1963 my Uncle Lou took me to West Brom. It was my first game. I was ten.

It was one of the most famous days in football, which, for those of you who may not know, did actually exist before the Premier League came along to save us all in 1992. All the games kicked off at three o'clock and here are the results:

Blackpool 1	Chelsea 5
Burnley 6	Manchester United 1
Fulham 10	Ipswich 1
Leicester 2	Everton 0
Liverpool 6	Stoke 1
Nottingham Forest 3	Sheffield United 3

Sheff. Wednesday 3	Bolton 0
West Brom 4	Tottenham 4
West Ham 2	Blackburn 8
Wolves 3	Aston Villa 3

Sixty-three goals in ten games, watched by a total of just over 293,000 people. There was a standing joke in the days when players happily trained on suet pudding and cigarettes that games around Christmas were always affected by possible over-indulgence on their part. The results on Boxing Day might indicate that there was some truth in this. The corresponding fixtures also took place during the holiday period and so it happened that two days afterwards, Saturday the 28th, the same matches (almost, as will be revealed) yielded another 36 goals in ten games. Ipswich exacted a degree of revenge for their double-figure spanking, but Blackburn, despite remaining top of the table, had clearly shot their bolt during their jaunt in the capital and contrived to lose at home to West Ham. Liverpool, who didn't play on the 28th, eventually won the league. They will resurface in this chapter.

Of the 20 clubs who featured on Boxing Day, half, at the time of writing, play in the Premier League. Four clubs currently in the top flight were plying their trade in the third and fourth tiers of English football in the winter of 1963/64: Palace, Watford and Bournemouth in the third, Brighton in the fourth. The First Division consisted of 22 clubs in 1963. So, ten games on Boxing

Day, ten on the 28th, but the eventual champions (and Stoke) didn't play the reverse fixture. Which two clubs are missing from the list?

Arsenal, obviously. And, maybe not so obviously, Birmingham City.

Let's be clear here. As I wrote to my cousin on the death of my Uncle Lou, I knew exactly what his father was up to. Some years earlier I had, for reasons which are hard to fathom, declared that I was a Blues supporter. My mother was recently widowed, and I had two older sisters who couldn't care less about football. I was alone and unguided in the world of affiliation. My Uncle Lou was trying to save me. I always give him a little nod when I visit his grave.

The game at the Albion was a cracker. Eight goals, a crowd of over 37,000, two goals from the legendary Jimmy Greaves. On a gloomy, cold winter's day, the floodlights were on well before half-time. This is exactly how you're supposed to fall in love with football. And I did. I wanted more.

I went home and told my mother how much I'd enjoyed it and that I wanted to go again. To see the Blues. This now requires some explanation.

I was ten years old and I had no one to go with. Uncle Lou had given salvation his best shot but he had a family of his own to attend to. My sisters liked hairdos, rock and roll and boys, and even though they were as supportive as any older siblings might be, there were some steps that were demonstrably too far. But the past is definitely a different country. I possessed an encyclopaedic knowledge of all bus routes around south Birmingham and was lucky to have lived in an age when ten-year-olds were given an independence and freedom which seems eye-wateringly liberal by contemporary standards.

So off I went on 28 December to watch the Blues play the Arsenal. I've done as much research as I can but none of it has revealed with absolute certainty what any of this cost. What has lodged in my memory is that a child's fare from King's Heath to the top of Bradford Street was three old pence (1p), and I'm practically certain that entrance to the ground was one shilling and six pence (7½p) for a junior. I base this latter calculation on the fact that I distinctly recall from later visits to go and watch Blues' reserves (yep!) that the entrance was nine pence. So the whole lot was about 10p or two shillings.

Notwithstanding my bus knowledge, I wasn't entirely sure where to get off but was spared any anxiety by the fact that most of the passengers were bound for the same place as me. I travelled on the top of the number 50 which could have afforded me a view of the landscape – most of it pretty familiar until we passed Moseley Village – had it not been for the fact that it was against the law for anyone to clean the windows on buses in those days and, naturally, the top deck was reserved for smokers, most of whom went to it with tremendous will and determination. I sat in the fug among the hackers, waited for when they all got off and followed the flow.

I wasn't quite sure where I was going but felt entirely safe. It's probably almost impossible for a modern reader to imagine that a ten-year-old boy on his own in such a situation would not have evinced some interest, but these were different days. As an example, as I passed the various pubs (terra completely incognita as far as I was concerned) there were, as there would have been at any given time on any given day, kids sat on steps with either a bottle of pop or a packet of crisps. I'm not sure when things changed, but the spilling over into the streets of pub patrons was unknown and so kids were, literally, parked on steps while dads, and occasionally mums, went inside. Given that I have spent a significant proportion of my adult life on licensed premises, it is, perhaps, something of a surprise that the interiors of such places were then as mysterious and unknown to me as the chambers of the city of Atlantis. In short, kids were everywhere and unsupervised; nobody paid them much attention. There might be something to be said for it.

Although I lived in relatively genteel King's Heath, I was no stranger to some of the city's coarser quarters. For reasons that I've explained in other publications, I went to primary school in Balsall Heath. Even though I was blithely unaware of it at the time, this was at the heart of one of the poorest parts of the city which, even by the early 1960s, still bore the scars of wartime bombing on top of what was already desperate slumland. So the walk up the Coventry Road, under Brockhouse Bridge and up to the ground – which any old rough calculation now tells me I've done around a thousand times – made no impact on me whatsoever. Nowadays, my season ticket at St Andrew's is close to the assembled away supporters who dirge out with tedious regularity the observation that Birmingham's a shithole and they want to go home – a reflection made, it seems, by all such followings everywhere. Well, two thoughts. First, it's true that we're not stuck in some dull gentrified suburb or imprisoned in a sterile Lego box in a retail park on a distant ring road. Second – call this a shithole? You should have seen it 20 years after the Nazis bombed it and successive governments treated the people who lived here as expendable factory or cannon fodder. I'll give you shithole.

All of which is by way of saying that the walk up to St Andrew's through inner-city poverty was dominated by the sole thought that I was, at last, going to see the Blues. Nothing else mattered.

The crowd funnelled through gates at the top of the hill into the Spion Kop entrance. I was a well-read ten-year-old, highly versed in the ways of the football annual. I could read the words – well, the letters – but I had no idea how to squeeze some meaning from them. Spy On Cop? If you already know the origin, as I now do, then it's all a bit obvious, but to save you the bother of googling it, the naming of Kops at football grounds originated from the battle of Spion Kop in the second Boer War in 1900, fought on a steep hillside near Ladysmith in South Africa. When the Blues moved to St Andrew's in 1906, local people were invited to use their domestic rubbish as ballast and landfill on which the structure was developed. The weariness of the metaphor of being built on garbage has stood the test of time.

Up to this point I had been unwittingly shepherded by the momentum of the crowd, but once through the turnstiles there were decisions to be made. In front of me stood the imposing hill built on the landfill of the residents of Bordesley and even though some chose to turn left or right, I took my chances on the steep stairs right in front of me which seemed the most popular choice. At the top I could look down and see the pitch and so made my way down the still relatively empty terracing and found a spot some 12 rows back from the low brick wall which separated the concrete steps from the pitch. In the decades that followed, I spent two or three seasons watching from behind the goal at the Tilton Road end and bought my first season ticket as an adult in the rug-and-thermos Main Stand where my stepfather (not around in 1963) sat. But, basically, on 28 December 1963, I made my way down the Kop and stood between the halfway line and the Railway End and I've been there on and off for the last 56 years.

Occasionally, when watching the grainy, jerky footage of football from that era, I can genuinely feel and recall some of what it was like. One thing, however, will not and cannot be reproduced. The smell.

It's entirely true that football, even in its sanitised version in the second decade of the 21st century, still has its distinctive aroma. Flash, modern arenas have often dispensed with the irresistible salmonella wagons that should line the streets to grounds and, thank goodness, toilet facilities have improved beyond measure. Smoking has largely been eradicated from grounds (although, venture to the toilets in the away end at half-time lest you think the ban unbreachable) and modern hygiene reduces, but doesn't eliminate, your chances of being forcibly snuggled next to a rank sweatball. Nonetheless, there remains a smell to football – beer, sweat, onions, masculinity. Yet even at its worst, and it's an oddity that in the digital age of artificial intelligence we can't yet record smell in order to make comparisons, the modern ground would smell like the Hanging Gardens of Babylon when likened to its 1960s counterpart.

First, of course, was the fact that it was compulsory to smoke. As if the tobacco fug were not enough, St Andrew's backs on to a railway line, which in those days meant steam, which, in its turn, was belched out in great gouts over the lowly stand at one end of the ground. Then there were onions and fat emanating from kiosks in and around the ground. It was a smell with which I was familiar enough, having encountered it in the city centre which was dotted with small stalls selling curious meat products. It wasn't until I discovered the anaesthetising effects of alcohol on the desires of the palate years later that I ventured anywhere near such foodstuffs, so unremittingly vile was the stench. And hovering over this cocktail of fragrance was piss. Piss merits a special mention.

There were 23,239 people in attendance that day which, in a stadium built mainly for standing, rendered it much less than half full. I mention this because football has constructed any number of tales of crowds being so dense that, unable to move, spectators urinated into rolled-up newspapers or into the pocket of the poor unfortunate in front of them as an act of necessity. It may have taken place somewhere, but I never witnessed it. But piss there was – and plenty of it. That was because at the top of the Kop stood any number of blokes who were pissing against the corrugated iron wall from where their emissions streamed downwards in a steady flow. I remember being somewhat flummoxed by this. Surely there must have been properly designated pissing places? Yes. Over there. Under the scoreboard. Gents. Why was nobody pissing there? Where they should be.

As my life has moved on, I've found myself pissing in some pretty carefully constructed temporary urinals. At fun runs and festivals, fairly primitive but functional structures require gentlemen to piss into channels fashioned from cheap, plastic guttering. There's the odd bit of splish and splash and occasional leakage from carelessly fashioned joints (on the guttering, that is) but it's OK. It's not hugely pleasant but it does the job. Compared to the Gents in the corner of the Kop at St Andrew's in 1963, such places are like the porcelain-tiled privies of the spa rooms in Versailles. Rather than splodge into the officially sanctioned lavatory facilities, many chose to take their chances on the top of the Kop.

Along with the smoke, the steam, the curious meats and the piss was the smell of men. There were some women and a few girls but watching football was very much a male pursuit. In all honesty, I couldn't tell you that I thought the smell of men was particularly awful but it was definitely distinctive. Clothing was heavy, voluminous and often went for days unchanged in an era when the notion of using a washing machine once a day – if you had one – was unthinkable. Attention to fine personal hygiene was a thing of the future and one bath a week was the norm for most people in an age of greedy immersion heaters. We probably all hummed a bit and so what with all the other contributory pongs, going to football had its own very special bouquet which I encountered for the first time on that day.

The teams emerged. Both were wearing strips that bear a remarkable resemblance to the official first-team kits they wear today. In the days prior to football shirts being marketing opportunities, teams only changed if there was a genuine clash of colours. Magentas, lavenders and lemons were all shades of an unimagined future: teams wore red, blue or white unless they were Norwich or Plymouth. So out came the Blues in blue shirts, white shorts and white stockings. Yes, stockings. For that was the official nomenclature for socks in those days. The Arsenal (supporters of a certain age will always use the definite article when describing them) wore their classic red shirts with white sleeves. They were not title contenders and finished seventh in the league that year, which is about where they had been for the previous few seasons, trailing in the wake of their North London neighbours and the powerhouses of Ipswich and Burnley. They endured a few further seasons of mid-table anonymity – a status which I then didn't appreciate I would rarely enjoy as a Blues supporter – before emerging in the 1970s as regular trophy winners. But in 1963, they were no great shakes.

On a dull, cold afternoon on a half-full, piss-drenched, stinky Spion Kop I watched with, I would like to think, a sense of prescient foreboding of the decades to come, as the Arsenal breezed to a 4-1 victory. I can't check all the fine details because the wonderful 11v11 website, which has sucked away so many of my evenings and on which this book is heavily reliant for factual accuracy, lists neither the Birmingham team nor its solitary goalscorer. Another source reveals that it was Alex Harley – and, yes, you might have thought I'd remember the scorer of the first Birmingham goal I witnessed. The details of the Arsenal line-up and their scorers are there in full. That must be telling us something.

At half-time one of the mysteries of life was revealed to me. I had seen something that had always puzzled me when assiduously studying my beloved football annuals. Forming the background to the photo of the leaping centre-forward – looking, to modern eyes, as though he was 47 if he was a day – were large capital letters on the perimeter of the pitch. I had no idea what they were for. Then, at half-time, numbers, which clearly corresponded to football scores, were slotted next to the letters. At that point, I realised that the large capital letters corresponded to other fixtures being played and that to know what was going on you needed to have purchased a programme. Just to make it entirely clear to anyone under the age of 30 reading this, I'll try not to shout – this was the only way you knew what else was going on. At the end of the game the new-fangled transistor radio would come into play and as we trudged back down the hill to the bus stop, you could huddle next to the plutocrat with such a device pinned to his ear should you feel the need to do so.

One result, however, would be known. As you were leaving the ground, everyone, but everyone, knew how the Villa had got on. Via the transistor radio or, on occasion, via the public address system (he only announced it if they'd lost), you'd know. I'll return to both subjects – the Villa and finding out results – later on.

So my first visit to St Andrew's ended in defeat. Among the many new experiences of the day was the numb frozenness of my feet by the end of the game.

It took some time for the blood to flow as I made my way under the Jeff Hall scoreboard, past the Augean stables of the Gents and back to the number 50s lined up in their numbers in the days when the bus was the principal form of transport for most supporters. I have friends, about whom I do worry, who can tell you exactly how many defeats they've seen, how often we've lost against various teams and the number of grounds where they've seen us beaten. I admit that it's not much of a boast to say that I can't do that, but I'm not quite so obsessive. And, to be analytically honest, it was probably best that my watching career set the tone for the future as it did.

I can't say with any certainty where I absorbed the notion that you stick with your team through thin and thinner, although it is fair to say that the caricature of the perennially pessimistic, unimpressed Brummie has its basis in hundreds, if not thousands, of Birmingham people I know. Anyhow, I acquired it. I knew you had to stick at it. I'm not sure whether my mother was waiting for my homecoming with the sort of fractious anxiety that in later parental life characterised my own restless sleep prior to late-night teenage return, but she merely asked how the Blues had got on and fed me. I asked if I could go again next week – it was an FA Cup game – and she agreed.

I want to tell you it was better. I want to tell myself it was better. We were playing Port Vale. At home. They were in the Fourth Division.

Birmingham City 1, Port Vale 2. Foggy. Smokey. At one point, steam from the railway, along with the fog, obscured the whole thing. Cold. Piss. Stinky. And, just so the point is not lost, the FA Cup was a big, big thing. If it's an ill wind that blows no one any good, then one of the few consolations was that my widowed mother with three children to keep was blissfully unaware of the damage that I was about to inflict on myself for the rest of my life and so when I came home to relay this most shocking of results, I'm delighted to say – even more so in retrospect – that it had no impact on her whatsoever.

If what happened in the two games that I first witnessed was typically ominous, the events of the next few weeks established a pattern with which I became only too familiar. Having been beaten at home by Port Vale, the Blues went to Old Trafford on the following Saturday and beat the mighty Manchester United, 2-1. Once again, it's worth making the point that the first you'd have known about this was the teleprinter laboriously typing out the result on the TV at about 4.45. To a ten-year-old in 1964, Old Trafford was about as accessible as the moon and so one could only, literally, imagine what such an event could have been like. I was both overjoyed and somewhat miffed: I'd been lumbered with two miserable, cold defeats. Why couldn't I have witnessed the good stuff? Still, I supported a team that could beat Manchester United away. That had to be a good thing. Didn't it?

In the next ten games, Birmingham City managed two draws and cemented their place in the bottom two places assigned for those teams to be relegated to the Second Division. I wasn't allowed to go to every home game, but in the middle of this dismal run I was charged with taking my eight-year-old cousin to a game, what with me being such an old hand at it and all that. I didn't like him. He was snively and didn't really want to come and Blues lost 2-1 to Sheffield Wednesday. Any faint hint of joy was a distant chimera and even two months into my active supporting career, I was beginning to get the hang of how to endure low expectations, leavened only by moments and episodes of unexpected delirium.

There was the possibility of just one such moment on Saturday, 28 March when, after 15 minutes or so, we were 3-1 up against Chelsea. We went on to lose 4-3 but, in many ways, that's not the interesting part of the story. That Saturday was during Easter weekend and on the following Monday we played the reviled neighbours on their own patch. Going to Villa Park, which later became a routine part of my weekend, was a two-bus job (50 into town, 39 out) and so just a step too far for my mum to give her permission. Astonishingly we won, 3-0, and then – and I checked all of this very carefully – we played them again the next day at St Andrew's and drew 3-3. Just the three matches in four days, then. It would have been nice to think that the three points (two for a win, one for a draw – as it was until 1981) gleaned from our neighbours gave us some sort of buffer against impending relegation. It did not, of course. In the succeeding three matches we conceded ten goals without reply, losing all of them. And so, in my very first season, I encountered the football supporting scenario that came to typify my allegiance to Birmingham City. It's April, the evenings have lengthened and the chill air has softened a little. And Blues go into the final week of the season with their fate – promotion or relegation – in the balance and, usually, with the odds stacked against them.

The club most frequently relegated from the various divisions is Notts County. Days before I wrote this, they experienced catastrophic demotion from the Football League, their 17th experience of such failure. Along with their 13 promotions they outdo Blues in terms of yo-yoism but for promotion to, and relegation from, the first flight of English football, we are matchless, having achieved both feats on 12 occasions. Since that fateful day in December 1963, there have been seven such relegations along with a further two from the second to third tiers, and eight promotions. So that's 17 seasons out of 55 where movement between divisions took place. On 12 occasions, survival or promotion was ensured in the final game. In the last six years alone, survival from the second tier was achieved on the last day and so when you stir in five appearances (one successful) in the play-offs since 1999, it's easy to see why the rites of spring around the B9 postcode tend to be rather fraught.

On 17 April West Ham beat Birmingham City 5-0, leaving the latter bottom but one in the table and three points behind Bolton Wanderers. Bolton had one more game to play – at home to mighty Wolverhampton Wanderers – and Blues two. The first of these was a midweek home game against Liverpool, who had just won the league. Much as I pleaded, I was not allowed to go to a night game during the school week. I can't remember how I found out the result. It could easily have been from the next morning's papers, but the newly anointed champions may have had a night or two on the brown ale and Blues had won 2-1. With an inferior goal average (don't ask – the more complicated forerunner of the more sensible 'goal difference'), we now had to beat Sheffield United and Bolton lose to Wolves. Both teams were at home.

All printed records clearly show the two games being played on separate dates, although I have no recollection of this. Bolton seem to have played on the Friday and our glamorous cousins from the Black Country had given them a good hiding, 4-0. I have no memory of this being the case – a situation unthinkable for us in the days of wall-to-wall TV coverage with split screens and multiple commentary teams. By contrast, however, I can recall the events of Saturday, 25 April 1964 with all the firmness and certainty of memory that now eludes me when I'm marooned in a supermarket aisle with not the first inkling of what I'm supposed to be looking for.

Before I describe what happened on that day – or at least, the one seminal moment – another brief bit of context is required. Substitutes were first introduced in English football at the beginning of the 1965/66 season. Up until that point, if your team was disadvantaged by someone being seriously injured and unable to continue, then it was just tough luck; you played on with ten men, or nine or whatever. Once substitutes were allowed, they were only permitted in case of injury, not for tactical purposes, and it was strictly one per game. You may well be ahead of me here, but this is important information for you to know prior to events at St Andrew's on 25 April 1964 with Birmingham City needing to beat Sheffield United to ensure their First Division survival.

All the trawling of the internet available has not been able to tell me the exact timing of the first of Birmingham's goals in what turned out to be a comfortable 3-0 win. It doesn't matter. There are some things stamped like a deep, red-hot brand into your consciousness.

One thing is for certain; the goal was scored as the result of a corner at the Railway End, right in front of me. The scorer was Trevor Smith, one of the few Blues players of his era – or any other come to that – who played for England. In the days when you had one centre-half per team whose job was to head, tackle and kick the ball into touch, Trevor was unfortunate to be playing at the same time as the dashing Billy Wright from up the road at Wolves. Wright played 105 times for England and was married to a pop star, so unglamorous, solid Trevor had to content himself with just two appearances. He was old school in every sense. After his 365 appearances for Blues, he played a dozen times for Walsall before opening a pub. He scored three goals and I saw one of them on that day in April 1964.

In goal for Sheffield United was Alan Hodgkinson. He only ever played professionally for the one club, turning out for them on 576 occasions. Like Trevor, he gleaned a few England caps in an era when competition for his place was fierce. To watch footage of how goalkeepers were unprotected fair game during this period is to spend pretty well all one's time wincing and flinching. They survived entire games being knocked, barged and charged before smilingly trotting off the pitch for a nice cuppa and a smoke. To have played 576 times in such conditions required tremendous physical fortitude. But however well prepared he may have been for any eventuality, nothing could have prepared poor Alan Hodgkinson for a fired-up Trevor Smith lumbering up for a corner as he approached the end of his career and with a relegation scrap to win.

As the corner came into the box, ball, Smith and Hodgkinson all ended up in the net together. Whether or not Smith was making any attempt to make contact with the ball, no one will ever know for certain …

and here I make no apology for another important digression. In an age where betting on a sending off is an entertaining punt for any watching neutral, it is difficult to imagine how rare such an event was back in the early 1960s (which, incidentally, is another reason to watch in wonder as Rattín was famously dismissed in the World Cup against England in 1966). It was a complete rarity and, as a consequence, Trevor was not sanctioned in any way and, even more bizarrely, the goal stood. The story does not end there.

Inured as he must have been to constant physical buffeting, Hodgkinson stayed on the ground. Players in 1963 didn't do that unless they were hurt. I once heard the late Jimmy Armfield, who could have counted himself unlucky not to have been England's first-choice right-back in 1966, ruefully observing an incident on which he was co-commentating on the radio. On seeing a player writhing and rolling, Armfield sorrowfully observed that if another player of his era had genuinely hurt him, the last thing he would have done would have been to let him know. Hodgkinson belonged to that same era – and to the one that didn't yet allow substitutes. In another way in which the sanitised, modern game is inferior to its forebears, the brilliant spectacle of an outfielder going in goal is now far too rare. But that is what happened that afternoon at St Andrew's as the Blues coasted to a 3-0 win against ten men with a stand-in keeper and so assured First Division survival.

I went home elated. We had survived; squeaked home by the skin of our teeth. My mother smiled and was pleased for me. One year later we were relegated to the Second Division where we remained for the next seven seasons. It was to be the first of nine relegations, so far, on my watch. I'm not sure whether, if I'd known this was to become an occupational hazard, I'd have bailed out at that point.

I think I'm glad I didn't.

Chapter 2

I realise that we may not be the sort of club that wins stuff

THE RELEGATION in April 1965 came at the end of my first year in secondary school. We remained in that division until a year after I left and had completed the first year of my undergraduate degree. Just for the record, we went up in 1975, not down.

Football support in my secondary school was much more of a mixed bag than I was used to. For those in the know, I went to King Edward School, Edgbaston (as a scholarship boy, not fee paying, before you ask) which brought in boys from beyond the immediate area of central Birmingham. Hence, as well as Blues and Villa (with the latter in the majority) there were plenty of Albion fans – the first I had encountered since dear old Uncle Lou – and some, rather exotically to my mind, who had thrown in their lot with Walsall. Blues fans were a definite minority and this must have been a reflection of the class composition of those who attended: Birmingham City was, and resolutely remains, a working-class football club. So here I was again, by no means on my own, but part of a group of near-oddities, surrounded by people with real expectations that their team might win things. And, to be perfectly fair, I counted myself among their number for a while.

As it happens, I had missed a sort of famous victory. In 1961, the Football League established its own cup, which many top teams didn't deign to enter. The first two-legged final in 1961 saw the Villa beat Rotherham, watched by just over 42,000; the following year, 30,000 people watched Norwich beat Rochdale over two games and then we had a go. Although nearly 70,000 saw us beat the Villa over two legs in May 1963, any wider recognition to be gained from this could not have been more underwhelming. There was no TV coverage, the final games were played in midweek at the end of the season and frankly, my dear, no one gave a damn. There was no European football to be gained (Europe? Football?) and if it was covered on the one midweek TV sports programme around at the time – *Sportsnight* – I wouldn't have seen it because it was too late on a school night. I remember it being reported in the local paper and being pleased and that was about it.

In 1967 things changed. The Football League, probably recognising that they had created a hopeless non-starter, managed to arrange that the final would be at Wembley and a place in the UEFA Cup – the third most important European competition after the European Cup and the Cup Winners' Cup – would be on offer. Once again, readers from the modern era may need a few words of explanation about getting to Wembley ... or maybe not. With play-off and lower-league finals attracting huge, near sell-out crowds, it is clear that getting there and seeing your team has an enduring appeal. The chances of seeing your team there have increased as a consequence of this wider use. Back in 1967 when this more democratic access to the place was a thing of the future, you would dream, literally, of seeing your team at Wembley. As a consequence, almost all teams decided that the League Cup was now a competition worthy of consideration. In 1967 Blues were trundling through a mediocre season in the Second Division – we finished tenth – but flirted (albeit with no satisfactory consummation) with cup success in both the FA and League Cups.

Two dreadful thumpings in both competitions put paid to any hope of glory.

The League Cup Final was to be played then, as it is now, in the early spring. The semi-finals, which Blues had managed to reach, were played in January and February. We drew Queens Park Rangers from the Third Division – one below ourselves – over two legs, the first at St Andrew's. On a school night. That's important to remember – not because by then it was rare for me to be allowed to go to night games, but because I had to go to school the next morning.

We were beaten 4-1 – at home – by a QPR team inspired by the precocious talent of a relatively unknown Rodney Marsh. And it had been on the telly. There's no need to go into details; it was as grim as it gets and if you're a supporter reading this, you'll have your own nightmares to bury. Three weeks later, QPR finished the job with a further 3-1 victory. The fact that they then went to Wembley (ggrrrr) and dramatically beat West Brom of the First Division 3-2 after being two goals down was no consolation whatsoever. We'd had our chance and blown it. But had we?

A few weeks after the utter catastrophe of the home defeat to QPR, a kind draw had seen us sneak into the fifth round of the FA Cup – the real cup. The way in which the importance of this brilliant cup competition has waned has been done to death, so this is not the place to rehearse some pretty weary old arguments. Suffice it to say that when you got to the last 16 of the competition, you were in the proper spotlight, especially if you were a mediocre Second Division club and you had the fortune of a home draw against the Arsenal. As with my first visit to St Andrew's a few years earlier, our opponents were not yet massive high-flyers. Nonetheless, they finished seventh in a league of 22 that season, so Arsenal at home was still big-time stuff. At nearly 14 years of age I was insufficiently embittered and tempered by decades of disappointment to see this not as a potential further embarrassment that might put even the QPR debacle into the shade, but could actually contemplate an unlikely giant-killing – like other clubs seemed to be able to do.

With 40,000 others, the vast majority of whom were, like me, to be standing on the terraces, I trooped up the hill to St Andrew's. The smoke, the curious meat smell, the piss and the sweat were magnified in the crush and I even found myself elbowed out of my normal spot – which had by now become a meeting place for some of my schoolmates, most of whom were Blues fans (I'll explain later). I moved along to the corner of the Kop and the Tilton Road, where I liked the greater volume of noise and the edginess of a spikier sort of supporter. Spikier because even before the advent of the noticeable, semi-organised, low-level hooliganism of the 1970s – I'm not referring to the world of 'firms', so beloved of creaky budget film-makers – there was, potentially, territory to be defended.

I said that most of the boys I went with were Blues fans. Not all. I'll explain.

In 1967 it would have been possible, in theory, for anyone, bearing whatever colours, to stand or sit where they wished. The segregation of crowds by affiliation was a thing of the future. 'Colours', incidentally, would have been the wearing of a hat or scarf or even the sporting of a rosette. The replica shirt had not yet seen the earth's light to line the deep pockets of the world's merchants. Overcoats, macs and jackets remained resolutely brown and made of the thickest, heaviest materials available. Sometimes they were vaguely waterproof. Logos did not adorn these functional garments.

In reality, most away fans gravitated towards each other to sing and chant, but it was commonplace for smaller groups or individuals to take up positions wherever they fancied as long as they were prepared to face the ire and wrath of locals at tense moments, specifically at the scoring of goals. So even they tended to drift towards their own. By the 70s the phenomenon of 'taking an end' – invading your opponents' favoured terrace and driving them from it – had become part of the hooligan ritual, resulting in some genuinely shocking violence. It was this that prompted the authorities to introduce designated areas for supporters of different clubs. In the late 60s, however, things were more lax and although not yet enshrined in the doctrine of hooliganism, there still existed the potential for an invasion of your end. Hence the greater edginess on the Tilton. That Arsenal game gave me a taste for it and I stayed there for a couple of years until things turned much uglier and I returned to the Kop where my school friends were.

To repeat – most, but not all, of whom were Blues fans. King Edward School, Birmingham aped all the trappings, customs and idiocy of the English public school system, one of which was that we had to go to school on Saturday morning. This was a complete nonsense, especially if, like me, you played for the school for either or both of the two main sports of cricket and rugby. It meant that you'd trek into school on a Saturday morning, fidget through a meaningless hour or so of something or other and then either get on a coach or go and get changed to await the opposition. On Saturdays when such fixtures took place, there was the outside chance that an early start at home for rugby could possibly mean a dash to football in the afternoon (I'll come to where in a minute), although this was rare. On non-fixture days at school, another scenario took place that will seem beyond comprehension to a younger reader.

As a relatively well-off, independent football supporter in 2020, one of the few genuine pleasures of supporting Birmingham City is going to watch them away from home. Among the group of friends and acquaintances that join me in this endeavour, we have adopted the self-deprecating, but undoubtedly unoriginal, mantra of it being a good day out, spoiled only by having to watch the Blues. Car ownership, train services and some disposable income make this simple pleasure attainable. In 1967 this was a different matter. Away travel was impossibly glamorous.

So, during weeks when those of us who would usually be playing for school teams found ourselves free, we'd arrange to go to watch football on a Saturday afternoon, either at Blues ... or the Villa. Not West Brom because, as established by a tradition decades old, they were – and are still – always at home on the same

Saturday as the Blues; Sunday football was something else that was yet to happen. So we'd go, with our mates, to whoever was playing. To tell people not much younger than myself that I'd probably spend about one Saturday in six standing on the Holte End watching the Villa, and that some of those Villa supporters I went with would join me on the Kop from time to time, sounds like deranged rambling, but it's what we did. We didn't jump about when the opposition scored, but that's what we were urging them to do at every turn. One of my happiest memories in those football watching days was getting back on the 39 bus to town when the Villa had lost and to drink in their sullen disappointment and resentment.

But on 11 March 1967 I was separated from my peers and watched with delight and incredulity as we beat the Arsenal 1-0 with a Geoff Vowden header in the 83rd minute. There exists some wonderful footage of this game which, when watched with a modern eye, does make it look like something from another planet. And it did, indeed, have an other-worldly feel to it as I left St Andrew's on one of the first light afternoons of mid-March to wait impatiently for the cup draw which was to take place, as it always did, on Monday lunchtime on the Light Programme – to become Radio 2 some six months later. This necessitated the smuggling of a transistor radio into school, the upshot of which was that in the last eight of the FA Cup, our reward for beating the Arsenal was a home tie against

Spurs. Spurs. The Arsenal had been big time but Spurs were something else.

Spurs had won the cup in 1961 and 1962, on the first of those occasions cementing the almost impossible task in those times of completing the 'double' of cup and league. Every player was an international and up front were Jimmy Greaves and Alan Gilzean – still spoken of by Spurs fans as their most stylish and effective forward pairing. We may have scraped a giant-killing against the Arsenal, but this was a different proposition.

The 40,000 crowd for the Arsenal game grew to 51,000. Any search will find you footage of this game on 8 April 1967 and to watch it now is to marvel at a number of things. First, how – thank goodness – there were so few crowd tragedies in those pre-Hillsborough days and the Taylor Report that followed. The answer must lie somewhere in a collective consciousness that had been bred of looking after each other in genuine adversity, even in those unsentimental, less genteel days. All the same, it sends a shudder down the spine, even though we were all happily oblivious to potential disaster at the time. Second, it was a rough old game played on ropey old bumpy pitches. How the ballplayers of the day exerted any degree of control over their art is a marvel. Third, with a rough old caseball made of absorbent leather, goalkeepers eschewed anything as effete as gloves and if they did slump to such limpness, what they wore looked more suited to some gentle rose pruning rather than protecting their fingers from sinew twisting and bone crunching. None of which occurred to anyone at the time as we played our part as a crowd in what looks like, if the surviving footage tells an accurate tale, a fairly absorbing 0-0 draw, bringing credit to a Second Division side against one that would go on to finish third in the First.

Don't worry. If you've been paying attention and awaiting the second thumping promised earlier, it's on its way. And in another symbolic episode it occurred at my first ever away game – visits to Villa Park don't count – at White Hart Lane on the Wednesday following the original cup tie. FA Cup replays of this sort almost always occurred in the week immediately afterwards and by great good fortune, this was in the second week of the school Easter holidays. My older sister was at that time working as a schoolteacher and living in central London – such possibilities existed at that time – and so what could have been easier for a kid approaching his 14th birthday than to wheedle a treat out of his parents, hop on a train from New Street, visit his sister and negotiate the transport system to White Hart Lane (not easy, as some of you will know) to go and watch his team try to get to the semi-final of the FA Cup? Excitement, anticipation and sheer wonder doesn't even begin to cover it.

6-0.

Was there any sort of silver lining? Well, I thrilled to my first experience of away travel and I didn't have to face people in school next day. That's about it.

We had one more shot at getting to Wembley in the 1960s and it was genuinely thrilling. Yes. I did just use that term to describe the Blues but don't be afraid; you'll be anticipating how this chapter plays out and you'll be right. All the same, March and April 1968 were two amazing months to be a supporter of Birmingham City.

Our league form was such that there remained the outside possibility of promotion, but for the third time in just over 12 months, it was the glittering lure of cup glory, national recognition and a trip to what I now know to be an unremarkable suburb of North London that quickened our collective heartbeat. Two relatively easy ties against Leyton Orient and Halifax Town saw us drawn once again against the Arsenal on 9 March at historic Highbury, their home ground. A school Saturday. Miraculously, no school fixtures. But in London. So many logistical problems of which the most pressing was, of course, how to go to such a game – assuming we could even get there – while disguising school uniform and divesting ourselves of school bags.

I admit to being a person who automatically glazes over when other men, and this is a gender-specific trait, regale me with their cleverness in avoiding the A652 by cutting through Hicktown and using a roadside burger van that does the best sausage bap in greater Anglia, thus reducing their journey by 20 minutes (so that they can then do what, precisely?), but I'll give you the quickest of rundowns as far as my memory can retain events from some half a century ago.

Bomber jacket, sweater and Blues scarf in bag prior to school. School finishes at noon. Blazer and tie into locker; bomber jacket, sweater and scarf on. Dash down to catch any of the 61, 62 or 63 into town. 12.30 from New Street gets you to Euston at about 2.30. Four stops and one change on the tube, a dash to the ground, in at around 3.15 … and it's still 0-0! But not for very much longer as the Arsenal score soon afterwards and it looks as though the game is stumbling towards its inevitable conclusion. Although I'm mainly surrounded by my own kind, I encounter, as I did at White Hart Lane nearly a year earlier, the nauseating irritation of entitled fans enjoying what they think is their due at the expense of their backward provincial cousins – and my blood rises. And then, the impossible happens. We score a goal. Very, very late in the game. And it's Geoff Vowden with a header again.

If you look for this player in footballing records, you will find nothing remarkable. Vowden was a workaday pro who gave of his best whoever he played for, even though he committed the cardinal sin of moving from Blues to Villa – for a princely £12,500 – towards the end of his career. Nonetheless, it was extremely gratifying when researching this game to read a comment under the YouTube video from an irate Arsenal fan referring to 'bloody Vowden again'. So, thanks to bloody Vowden we had a replay to look forward to at St Andrew's the following Tuesday – 12 March, my late mother's 53rd birthday. I do hope I bought her a bunch of flowers and a decent present: what happened that evening certainly merited something special.

Football fans now have any number of locations, real and digital, on which they can express opinions and exchange inanities. Topics regularly include best player you ever saw, best match you ever attended and, of course, best goal you ever saw. Without a shadow of a scintilla of a sliver of doubt, the best goal I ever saw was scored that night by Barry Bridges for Birmingham City as we beat the Arsenal 2-1. I watched from my new home in the Tilton as the ball was crossed from the right and Bridges leapt, and while horizontal to the ground, executed a scissor kick that flew past the venerable goalkeeper, Bob Wilson, at the other end of the ground.

And here's the thing. There is no footage of it and no still photograph to capture the moment. The next day's *Birmingham Mail* had to resort to an artist's impression, frame by frame, of this thing of wonder. It's a disgrace for me to make such a comparison, but this happened over 50 years ago and the number of people who saw it, rather like people who saw real action in the world wars, are gradually dying out. There are one or two regulars who now sit near me at St Andrew's who saw it and who, like me, need to spend no time pondering the 'best goal ever' question. It lives in the memory and nowhere else and there it remains, one single instant of ecstatic, magical exhilaration – and, like I say, that's not usually the sort of language one associates with Birmingham City.

In the sixth round, the quarter-final, we were to play Chelsea at home. It's worth a brief digression to talk about Chelsea, particularly for younger readers, many of whom will have known nothing other than the club's quest for global dominance. They had won the First Division in 1955 but their subsequent record was patchy. They were relegated in 1962, albeit they came straight back up the following year. However, further relegations followed in 1975, 1979 – which resulted in a stay in the Second Division of five years – and then again in 1988, returning instantly again the following year. Their ground, Stamford Bridge, was shabby and ramshackle and, as is still the case, they were bedevilled by a certain section of support renowned for racism and violence. It's true that they also enjoyed the patina of glamour which spilled over from the more fashionable parts of west London and were often associated with a 'showbiz' allure, but as an entity, Chelsea was a far cry from its current corporatised brand. In 1968 though, they were doing well and finished the season sixth in the First Division.

The official record shows that 52,500 people attended that game. I was one of them and it's worth explaining how that was the case. What was clear about the Arsenal cup games in both 1967 and 1968 – both were pay on the day as was usual at that time – was that the ground was clearly filled beyond capacity. Whatever the official attendance figures said was a fib and, as must have often been the case in that pre-Taylor era, even the one-eyed, un-safety conscious authorities of the day must have realised the potential for calamity. The Chelsea game was, therefore, all-ticket. Listen now with wonder, if you will, about how such tickets were obtained at relatively short notice in those pre-internet, pre-credit card days.

Given that there were 18 days between the Arsenal replay and the Chelsea game, ticket sales must have taken place on either Sunday, 17 or Sunday, 24 March. The ticket office/turnstiles were to be open at St Andrew's at around nine – even my nerdy memory fails that test of precise recall. And so the only question to be answered was 'what time to get there to be sure of getting one?' I decided that four o'clock in the morning would be just about perfect; my mother was not convinced. My stepfather had a season ticket over in the rug-and-thermos stand, into which, as far as I could see, no one under 50 ever ventured and so was assured of a ticket. Our relationship was perfectly cordial if not hugely close and, fortunately, he fought my corner on the early start … except that he wasn't getting up at four o'clock in the morning on a Sunday to drive me there. He was a shift worker at the Longbridge car factory and sleep patterns were of great importance. However, as Brummies of a certain age will know, this was not an insuperable problem.

Night buses ran hourly from the Maypole to town and back. Problem solved.

I duly left the house on whichever Sunday morning it was at around 3.20 to get the 50 bus returning from the Maypole towards town, thinking that by going so early I would have stolen a march on the lie-abeds who'd be scrabbling around for the leavings later on. I was quickly disabused of this notion the moment I saw a queue – a queue – at the bus stop. At half past three in the morning. When it arrived, the bus was already half full and had reached capacity by the time it reached Bradford Street where we all trundled off, set off up the Coventry Road to be met by … a queue. A queue, stretching back a full quarter of a mile or so from the ground at four in the morning. And I was at the back of it – at least for the time being.

The story ends well in every respect – like I say, this is an atypical Birmingham City episode. At about 10.30 I purchased a ticket and made my weary way home. On Saturday, 30 March, we beat Chelsea 1-0, not bloody Vowden but Fred Pickering, and so reached the semi-final of the FA Cup. We had beaten two major First Division teams while hanging around the middle of the second tier. We had a real chance of getting to the final of the real cup. Bliss it was to be alive, to borrow from dear old Wordsworth, whose team never got a chance to go to Wembley, so how would he know? For the moment, only one question remained: who would we have in the semi-final and to which exotic neutral ground would it take us?

On the same day we beat Chelsea, Leeds beat Sheffield United and the Albion drew with Liverpool. Everton were to be the other definite semi-finalist. The cup draw, as ever, was on the Monday and it transpired that we were to play either Albion or Liverpool. The former seemed to have spurned their advantage by failing to win at home and so needed to face a replay at daunting Anfield. We had to wait another week as, for whatever reason, the replay did not take place until ten days afterwards. Albion and Liverpool played out another draw and so went to extra time and penalties ... no they didn't. Ten days after the game at Anfield, the tie went to a second replay at Manchester City's Maine Road ground – which is to feature grimly in the next chapter as well – where the Albion prevailed. A total of 163,335 people watched the three games, the last of which was on a Thursday, a rare event in those days.

No amount of research or getting old blokes to scramble around in their fading memories has been able to supply an answer to the question as to whether our replay was scheduled to be played at Villa Park prior to the Albion's qualification or not. Old Trafford was the obvious venue for Everton to play Leeds, but presumably, had Liverpool won, the game would have been played at Hillsborough. But they didn't and so there was to be an all-Birmingham semi-final played at Villa Park.

I'm never quite certain about referring to the Albion as a Birmingham club. Their ground, The Hawthorns, is less than five miles from Birmingham city centre, but there has always been an other-worldliness about them. Nonetheless, the bare facts were that this was going to be a very local affair indeed – and given extra spice by Albion's miserable visit to Wembley the year before where they lost to Third Division QPR. Now they had not-quite-so-lowly neighbours, who had seen off higher quality opposition from the First Division, who wanted to prevent them from going back. They were to go on to finish in eighth position at the end of the season.

The Albion played Liverpool in Manchester on Thursday, 18 April. The semi-final was to be played nine days later and so tickets were to be on sale at St Andrew's on Sunday, 21 April. By now, of course, I knew the drill … and, no, I was not going to get caught out by the fact that the Blues would have a smaller allocation at a neutral venue. The attendance at Villa Park the following Saturday turned out to be just under 61,000, so I'm assuming clubs got around 30,000 each as opposed to the 40,000 or so that would have been available for the two previous home ties. Never mind the 3.20 bus; I was going an hour earlier.

This time I was not fazed by the fact that others were at the bus stop, even at this earlier hour. But I did notice that the bus was fuller than last time and that as it progressed it went sailing past stops where others were waiting. This looked and felt different and this sense was confirmed once I got off. The queue to the ground was clearly longer than last time and because I was 15 years old and encumbered in life only by the fact that I knew everything there was to know about anything and that, conversely, my parents slouched through life somehow managing to get by shrouded in darkest ignorance, I had shunned my mother's offer to make me some sandwiches and a flask. It was going to be a long night – and it got even longer when, at about 10.30, the queue in front of me broke up as news filtered through that all tickets were sold.

Who came to my rescue? Why, Uncle Lou, of course.

Uncle Lou owned a draper's shop on the Stratford Road and enjoyed a varied social life: he was well connected. Prior to my mother's remarriage four years earlier he had been supportive and helpful to our family and, of course – see previous chapter – had tried to save me from myself by taking me to the Albion. My obsession with football had always been a source of some bemusement for my mother but she had tolerated it as largely harmless and having the bonus of keeping me occupied. By a stroke of luck, her second marriage was to a Blues supporter and, as a consequence, she clearly felt it in her better interest to at least feign some kind of genuine attention. This meant that my failure to get hold of a semi-final ticket did, in fact, register with her more firmly than it might have done a few years previously. It must have been she who approached Uncle Lou as there was little love lost between him and my stepfather – not a matter for this particular book.

On either the Wednesday or Thursday of that week, Uncle Lou came up with the goods – and I don't want to sound ungrateful when I add an 'almost' to that. Blues had been allocated standing in the Holte End – a delicious irony that we should occupy our neighbours' stronghold. Albion were to be in the uncovered Witton End at the opposite end of the ground. I'm sure you're ahead of me here, so I won't spell it out in full; that's where Uncle Lou's precious ticket was for. All the same, I was in. I had a ticket. I have no idea whether or not school had fixtures on that day but whatever happened, I was going.

Looking at the various bits of footage that exist, my recollections that we gave them a pretty good game seem to be confirmed. Bloody Vowden hit the post but we failed to score and the Albion did so once in either half and so went to Wembley and this time they won, beating Everton 1-0 with another goal from Astle in extra time. It meant that he had scored in every round of the FA Cup which is quite an achievement. Jeff Astle remains a genuine Albion legend, not just for the goals he scored but for his family's continuing, dogged campaign to investigate the deleterious effects of concussion and head injuries suffered in all sports. He seems to have been modest and self-effacing and even enjoyed temporary fame as a crooner on the early

TV *Fantasy Football* programmes. So it's kind of a shame that most of us remember him for missing a sitter against Brazil in the 1970 World Cup and for Blues fans, as the man whose efforts stopped us getting to Wembley.

These had been almost glorious years, even if they only delivered inglorious failure. We weren't done, though. Blues got to FA Cup semi-finals twice in the next seven years and there are tales to follow. All the same – here's the spoiler alert. We never got to Wembley.

The picture was definitely becoming very clear: we didn't look like a side that won stuff.

Chapter 3

We flirt with competence and become almost attractive

BLUES BUMBLED about in the late 1960s and early 70s, eventually achieving promotion in May 1972 at a hair-raising game on a Tuesday night at Leyton Orient. We'll return there shortly: no Blues history would be complete without an account of that evening. Two weeks prior to this game we had another shot at FA Cup glory, but this time the mighty Leeds United were our opponents in the semi-final at Hillsborough and we were soundly beaten 3-0. Leeds went on to win the cup, beating the Arsenal in the final.

There is a peculiar coda to this episode in our history and one which even the most ardent and obsessed of Blues historians tend to forget. It involved playing in a third-place play-off, which was an experiment put in place by the FA between 1970 and 1974. Having tried several formats for this odd, unwanted fixture, it was decided to have it as a pre-season warm-up, and in early August 1972 the game against the other losing semi-finalists, Stoke, was played at St Andrew's. It ended in a draw and was decided by the new-fangled method of the penalty shoot-out, which Blues won. The shoot-out was the first ever in the FA Cup and it divided opinion. *The Sunday Times* condemned it as a 'coconut shy ritual' and the FA shelved it as a device for the next 20 years. So I'm not sure if that makes us trailblazers or not.

In the semi-final proper, our best effort at goal came, inevitably, from the prodigy, Trevor Francis. The game was played on my 19th birthday and I mention this not from the need to put myself needlessly at the centre of the picture, but to point out that it was four days prior to Trevor's 18th. Incidentally, he's always, always just plain Trevor.

As years pass by it has become inevitable that those who play sport at the highest level are significantly younger than me. Trevor was the first to set the trend. He had made his debut in September 1970 and later in that season, still at 16 years of age, he scored all four goals in a home win against Bolton. Just at the point of writing this, a new wonder boy, Jude Bellingham, has beaten Trevor's age record. All the same, here was a life-changer for me: a bloke playing for the Blues who was younger than me. My own playing prowess never took me beyond old-fashioned, kick, bottle and bite parks football and so I harboured no illusions about success in that area, but a 16-year-old scoring four goals at St Andrew's would have screwed the lid immovably on any such fantasies.

In the previous chapter I explained how Birmingham fans of a certain age never have to ponder the best Blues goal they have ever seen – Barry Bridges, Arsenal, FA Cup replay. The same applies to best player to wear the shirt – and my apologies here to the over-70s who can remember the team of the 50s who did OK. From time to time the name of Christophe Dugarry is flirted with and it is true that in his brief period he was, at times, jaw-droppingly scintillating. He also tended to fall over a lot when he hadn't been fouled and Blues fans didn't like that, but he soon got the picture. He would only pass the ball to the wonderful Stan Lazaridis or the redoubtable Geoff Horsfield – watch the footage if you don't believe me – but he was, as befits a World Cup winner, a pedigree in with the street dogs and shone accordingly.

But to compare him with Trevor? Trevor who played 319 times for us, scoring 130 goals, as compared with Dugarry's 30 appearances and six goals, even though he once won a game pretty well on his own (Southampton at home, 2003). There is no case to be made.

At the beginning of 2019, the football media celebrated 40 years since the first £1 million transfer in English football. Even given the propensity of the supporters of provincial, mediocre teams to incubate imagined grievances about mainstream coverage, it was an infuriating episode. All concentration was on the brilliance of Brian Clough in boldly using someone else's money to acquire the player who went on to guide Forest to European glory and then on to international stardom. Hardly a mention of the club that had nurtured and developed him for the previous eight years. It was up to Trevor himself to do so in the endless interviews on the topic – a welcome, proper intervention noted by all Blues fans at the time. There is video testament aplenty to his talents but none of it can capture the thrill of being there on a dank afternoon or a floodlit evening and seeing a skinny kid sidle past the choppers and hackers on the mudbath pitches of that era.

In 1996 Trevor, on the back of a reasonable managerial career, came back to manage the Blues for five years. On reflection, it is unlikely that anyone other than someone so firmly sutured into the club's history and culture would have been given that long. He guided us to the League Cup Final in 2001 when we were still in the Second Division where, but for an egregious refereeing error by the bumptious David Elleray, we would have beaten high-flying Liverpool (it was in Cardiff, by the way; Wembley, for major finals, at least, remained unattainable). We reached the Second Division play-offs on three occasions under his tutelage, failing hopelessly on all occasions. Once, in 2000, we somehow contrived to lose the first leg at home to Barnsley 4-0, having lost on penalties, 7-6, the previous year to Watford. The following year we had another go. Another disaster. And one that requires recalling in some detail. We played Preston North End.

Blues had won the first leg 1-0 on Sunday, 13 May and the second was to be played at Preston's Deepdale ground the following Thursday. Let's just get the cliché out of the way – it's the hope that kills you. Preston scored just before the half hour, but on the hour itself Geoff Horsfield levelled to put us 2-1 up on aggregate. And then they get a penalty, to be taken by a bloke who hasn't missed one all season. He walks up and smashes it against the bar and we're still 2-1 up and we must be going to Cardiff for the final now. As Preston push ever harder for an equaliser, a series of reasonable chances come our way, none of which are taken. What happens at the end of the game can only happen in live, unscripted sport.

We break. Stan Lazaridis nips past the keeper and, honest boy that he is, avoids the temptation to step into the keeper's flailing attempt to tackle him and get a penalty. Stan – just fall over!! He doesn't. He shoots. His shot beats the keeper and hits the outside of the post. The ball somehow stays in play and runs away to the Preston full-back who gets it upfield and they score a goal in the 92nd minute of the game. Extra time passes in the usual nondescript blur of timid, non-committal neutrality and we drift towards penalties. This does not turn out to be Trevor's finest hour.

There ensues an altercation between Trevor, the referee and anyone else who wants to put in their two penn'orth about the end at which the penalties are to be taken. This appears to the uninvolved bystander to do nothing other than discomfit the Blues players in particular. Some three months earlier most of them had been involved in the failed shoot-out in the League Cup Final against Liverpool – a moment that produced a touching, iconic photograph of Trevor paternally embracing a young Andrew Johnson who had missed the final penalty. It's all a bit chaotic and it seems to transfer to the players, the first two of whom, Marcello and Purse, miss. Preston duly win the shoot-out and we trudge miserably down the M6. Preston lose in the play-off final to Bolton, who remain in the Premier League for the next 11 years before embarking on their current damnable road to basket casery. Trevor is eventually sacked the following autumn and the next season his opposite number at Preston, David Moyes, embarks on his successful career at Everton. There is joy to come for the Blues, but not on Trevor's watch … so let's return to events at Brisbane Road in May 1972.

A sensational run of results from the turn of the year in 1972 was built largely around an attacking nexus of Trevor, Bob Latchford and Bob Hatton – all of whom were supplied by flying winger Gordon Taylor – yes, he of the gargantuan salary in his role as lugubrious representative of the players' union. Behind them was flashy midfielder Alan Campbell, along with the only one of the regulars not to sport a fashionably long mane offset by some sort of pre-hipster facial hair, the sternly military centre-half, Roger Hynd. Hynd, who died a couple of years ago, would make any modern so-called 'no-nonsense player' look like an effete ice skater in a tutu. He was proper hard. And this was in an era when 'making your mark' on your opponent in the first couple of minutes was a) mandatory and b) unofficially sanctioned by officials who, basically, considered it all part of the game. Decked out in the famous penguin shirt, Blues were a formidable outfit and the cup run that ended in the Leeds defeat had not impeded our gradual rise up the table.

The last full round of Second Division fixtures was played on Saturday, 29 April but, because of the semi-final, we still had one more game to play. Again, this sounds bizarre when seen from the modern era but that's just how it was. At the end of the Saturday's fixtures (and, take note, we are still on two points for a win in 1972), Blues were one point behind Millwall, who had played all their games, in second place. Our goal average was superior, so a draw would do. Norwich were up as champions. So, just to recap – and take this in along with the growing rise in anti-social behaviour at football matches where official segregation and all-ticket league matches are as yet unknown – to gain promotion to the First Division, Birmingham City have to take a point from Leyton Orient at their ground in East London. Millwall, from East London, obviously need Orient to prevent this from happening and so they make their way in unlovely droves to their neighbours'

Brisbane Road ground the following Tuesday to make their feelings known. As do thousands of Birmingham City supporters, including me.

The current official capacity at the wonderful Brisbane Road ground is 9,271. The official attendance that night was 33,383, and it was estimated that at least 15,000 of these were Blues fans. Orient's average home attendance for the whole of the season, including this 33,383, was 10,817, so by any stretch of the imagination, some 8,000 Millwall fans had probably found their way in. It was cosy.

Blues go one better than the point needed, score as the hour approaches and hang on to win, spurred on by the raucous accompaniment of the travelling supporters. As the game drew to an end, Orient supporters sensibly began to make their way to their homes and still vacant boozers; they predicted a riot and one was very nearly served up. There is no footage of the game or of what followed, so I'll do my best.

At the final whistle, the players successfully managed to get to the dressing room – where they were captured huddled in the bath in a photo that, once again, belongs to a different world – and thousands of Blues fans invaded the pitch. When they got there, two things happened. First, a genuinely panicky announcement was made over the PA that there had been a bomb reported in the main stand and that everyone was to evacuate the ground immediately. Had such an announcement been made two years later after the pub bombings in Birmingham city centre, it's possible that this warning may have been given greater credence by tens of thousands of celebratory Brummies (if you're interested, I didn't go on the pitch. I have no idea why/why not, I just didn't). The warning turned out to be a hoax. So, second: thousands of Brummies on the pitch. At the other end, thousands of Millwall fans penned in by dozens of mounted police. Somehow – even though I'm sure there will be alternative tales of derring-do in the remaindered biography of some self-appointed king of the hoolies – the situation remained just about under control. We were promoted to the First Division, where we remained with nothing more than a couple of minor relegation scares, for the next eight years. We became almost OK; even before I'd reached my 20th birthday, I'd come to accommodate the fact that this was something to be celebrated.

Before we were relegated again in 1979 – and, yes, I do appreciate how this theme hangs like a gloomy spectre over our history – we finished tenth in the First Division, followed by a quick flirt with the drop at the end of 1974 (19th out of 22), then 17th, 13th twice and another heady 11th, before going down again in 1979 … only to come straight back up in 1980.

Perhaps the most startling of victories in that era occurred on 4 December 1976 at Leicester City's old Filbert Street ground. A cold, frozen start to the month meant that only five of the 11 fixtures in the First

Division went ahead. But before the tale unfolds, a word about *Match of the Day*.

In 1976 *MOTD* featured one game. The BBC did not reveal which game it was to be until all the fixtures had been concluded, which in those days was at about 4.48 on a Saturday at the absolute latest. Games kicked off at 3, there was no extra time at half-time – which lasted ten minutes (just enough time for the players to have a quick drag) – and any time added at the end of the game was entirely arbitrary. Very often refs would employ the same attitude as I did myself when refereeing schoolboy games: if it was obvious that one side was winning, just blow up and get off – you weren't doing anyone any good by hanging about. So, by the time the official results were being read on TV, or just after Herbert Bath's *Out of the Blue* had heralded *Sports Report* on the radio, the secret would very nearly be out. I wasn't at Leicester that day and was delighted to learn that of the five games actually played, ours had been chosen. We had won away which, in itself, was a cause for celebration. And we had won in style. 6-2. That is not a misprint. We had won away, 6-2. And we were going to be on the telly that night. That is happiness.

There is extensive footage of the game and it's very revealing. It appears to be taking place on an ice rink and not at all a game for the faint-hearted. At the centre of the drama was a player who was almost synonymous with fearlessness and hardness: Kenny Burns. Kenny always looked as though he might be hefting around an extra pound or two, although this only emphasised his bullish qualities on the field. He was Scottish and, in common with most of the tough Caledonian footballers of the day – and there were plenty, believe me – he resolutely refused the cosmetic improvement that might have been provided by the odd denture or two. He sported flowing, pre-Braveheart locks and was one of those players who, once the chalk line had been crossed, considered nothing important other than winning the game and battering anyone out of the way who might prevent that from happening. He could play with equally good effect as a centre-half or a centre-forward. On some days it was difficult to tell anyway.

Not to put too fine a point on it, it's clear even from the grainy video and from a distance of over 40 years that Leicester didn't really fancy it. Their keeper wore tracksuit bottoms which was by no means a rarity but still looks slightly odd. Beyond this detail, however, it is impossible to mention this reluctance of Leicester players to get stuck in on this treacherous surface without somehow seeing it as a precursor to one of the most famous sartorial decisions in the story of English football.

In January 1979, on another freezing day, Leicester winger Keith Weller decided to wear a pair of white tights under his shorts as protection against the cold and the ice. Weller had a distinguished career, playing at Chelsea and Tottenham as well as representing England on four occasions. However, stick his name into Google and immediately after his surname, the words 'white tights' will appear. All succeeding stories will bear mention of the tights. When he died in 2004 his obituary writers shared this common interest in the fact that during an FA Cup tie against Norwich on 6 January 1979 he wore a pair of tights. He also scored a pretty good goal that day and was, by all accounts, an interesting and enthusiastic character to have around. But his lot in life and death is to be remembered as the man who chose to wear a perfectly sensible undergarment on a bitter winter's day.

In December 1976, most Leicester players looked as though they would not have been comfortable in anything other than full-body arctic gear. A combination of Trevor's startling speed on the turn, some indifferent goalkeeping from tracky-bottoms boy and Burns's willingness to stick his daft head where danger and injury lurked meant that he scored three goals – all headers – and we were 6-0 up before easing off and permitting the home team to score twice towards the end of the game. My entire Saturday evening was spent in quivering anticipation and some reckless drinking which ensured that watching *Match of the Day* – now with slow-motion replays – was a genuinely treasured Blues memory.

At the start of the season and for reasons known entirely to himself, a local car dealer had promised any Blues player who scored the sixth goal in a game a Triumph TR7. I'll be honest and admit that I had always consigned this story to the unbelievable and apocryphal, but it didn't take a great deal of research in local newspaper archives to confirm that it was true and that ocular proof existed of this strange gift. According to Burns, he was tempted to take the car: 'even I might have been able to pull in a TR7' he told *The Scotsman* newspaper. Instead, in an act of collective solidarity befitting a man who had grown up with poverty and deprivation in Glasgow, he refused the car, took the insurance money that went with it, gave each of his team-mates £200 – 'to be fair, I can't win it without the rest of the team' – and gave a tenner for Christmas to all of the apprentices. Although posing proudly with his team-mates in the local press with the car, the story goes that Burns got in his Austin 1100, as Brummie a choice of car at the time as anyone could wish for, and drove home.

I don't know where Kenny Burns was living but we can be certain that it would have been pleasant, comfortable and just about as ordinary as it could have been. Between 1973 and 1977 Howard Kendall played for the Blues. He had been the youngest player to play in the cup final in 1964 and went on to become part of one of the most dynamic midfield partnerships with Colin Harvey and Alan Ball at Everton in the late 60s and early 70s. Almost unbelievably in the current age, when some English midfielders seem unable to pick a pass when going forward, Kendall never played for his country. He went on to enjoy a successful and varied managerial career and he was, without doubt, one of the best footballers I have seen playing for Birmingham City. He played for us 115 times and scored 16 goals. And I do know where he lived.

After 300 appearances in the top flight of English football, Howard Kendall lived in a solid, 1930s, three-bedroom house in a respectable suburb of south Birmingham. Handy for work, handy for training. I don't know what he drove, but I'm betting it was much more Austin 1100 than Triumph TR7. Other publications and biographies have dealt thoroughly with the notion that professional footballers were once very much part of their local communities so I'm not going to repeat that narrative. That players were, very properly, able to enjoy significantly better lifestyles with the abandonment of the maximum wage and those improvements to their contractual obligations is to be applauded. All the same, theirs was a life very different from that of their current counterparts.

It's true that notwithstanding lurid tales of great avarice and excess from modern stars, many of them acknowledge the hugely privileged nature of their position and make great efforts to contribute to wider society. One largely unsung benefit of players coming from around the world to play in England has been the influence of these young men who have borne witness to war, cruelty and deprivation on others who may have enjoyed a more cossetted path to success. Kenny Burns with his £200 windfall and Howard Kendall with his semi in Sheldon had something in common with such young men who have not forgotten where they come from.

But back to the mid-70s, and because it's Blues, on to the inevitable tale of failure and disappointment. If you're a Blues supporter, you know what's coming, so look away now or skip on to the next chapter (which isn't much jollier).

If you need proof that football's past is a different country, spend a few moments looking at the final First Division table in 1975. Here are just a few headlines. Derby County finished as champions fending off challenges from Liverpool, Ipswich and Everton. Close behind them at the top end of the table were Sheffield United, Stoke and Middlesbrough. Chelsea were relegated along with Luton and Carlisle; Tottenham narrowly escaped. Manchester United are notably absent from the final table having been relegated the year before, albeit they returned immediately. Perhaps the only note of conformity is that Blues nestled safely enough in 17th out of 22, four points clear of the danger zone.

Victories away at lowly Chelsea and Luton, followed by home wins against neighbours Walsall and then relatively high-flying Middlesbrough saw us into the semi-finals of the FA Cup for the third time in seven years. Our opponents were to be Fulham from the Second Division and, once again, we were off to Hillsborough. We had Trevor Francis, we were in the First Division and it was going to be third time lucky.

All they had were ageing England has-beens Alan Mullery and Bobby Moore.

We were reckoning without John Mitchell. In 1975 I had no idea who John Mitchell was. He was a workaday centre-forward playing in the Second Division. His professional playing career, which spanned from 1972 to 1981 before injury truncated it, yielded 75 goals from 251 games; 170 games for Fulham and 81 for Millwall. Two of his goals for Fulham were against Birmingham City. One was on 5 April 1975 at Hillsborough where the game finished 1-1; the other was in the 120th minute in the replay four days later at Maine Road, Manchester. It was a complete mess of a series of lucky rebounds and ricochets but it was enough to take Fulham to the FA Cup Final the following month. So good honest pro John Mitchell saw us off … and in later years I became good friends with his brother, Norman, in the shadow of whom I played some old-men's football and who, because he was a true gentleman, never made quite as much as he could have done about the fact that his brother ruined another FA Cup dream for me and tens of thousands of others. Fulham were beaten in the final by West Ham and dear Norman died a few months before this book was written. His brother is part of Birmingham City history but, given this post facto association, I can never bring myself to dislike him.

So, in the 70s we hung around as a fixture in the First Division and that was more than any of our neighbours managed to do, including the most loathed. We didn't achieve much and we didn't come remotely close to winning anything, even in those more democratic days when the provincial and the unfashionable could possibly grab their day in the sun. On a personal note, some aspects of my relationship with the Blues changed – and, yes, I am calling it a relationship; it's a lifelong commitment for better or for worse. By the mid-1970s I no longer lived in Birmingham and I was a kind of grown-up who was working for a living. I also chose to play football, at however low a level, rather than watch it.

This was a decision on which I look back from my sixties with great approval. It meant, however, that the weekly ritual of week in, week out watching was broken, even though I took every opportunity, even in the dog days of the 80s, to go home or away whenever I could. This absence from games brought with it the challenge that is another vestige of a bygone era: finding out the result.

I am now surrounded at games by people looking at telephones. Even when their team has scored a goal, the phone comes into play. Look, for example, at still photos taken moments after goals are scored. In the crowd there will be those who, at that very moment, choose to photograph the celebrations that are taking place on the pitch.

I think that what I am about to say will resonate with most of this readership. Whenever Birmingham

City score a goal I am, if I'm totally honest, just a touch surprised. It's not what I expect to happen. I've not been dedicated enough to research how many times I have witnessed Birmingham City scoring a goal but I'm going to take a rough guess at it being just over a thousand. And every time it happens, even though I go to the game with the sole, intense desire of seeing my team score as many goals as possible, I'm always faintly amazed that we manage to do so. With the rare exception of a fourth goal being scored as the icing on the cake, I celebrate most goals quite wildly and in a manner entirely unbecoming for a man of my age. At such moments of ecstasy (relax, I'm taking the image no further) the last thing I would think of doing is to try to take a photograph. Of anything.

All of which is by way of saying that we live in a world that is unimaginably removed from trying to get next to the bloke with the transistor radio to glean any updates. On a Saturday, unless you had been lucky enough to gather the scores from transistor man and if you were travelling by bus, you'd miss *Sports Report* on the radio and by the time you got home it was nearly time for *Doctor Who* or *The Monkees* on the telly. So you had to go out and buy an *Argus*. *The Sports Argus*. I had assumed that out there somewhere there must be a fully documented history of *The Argus* in particular, and the Saturday evening sports paper in general, but I was wrong. The digital age has probably ensured that we will never see its like again. An Early Day

Motion in the House of Commons condemning the decision of Trinity Mirror to put *The Argus* out of its misery attracted a measly 17 sponsors and the motion itself appears to have slithered down the plughole of parliamentary procedure, never to resurface. It was an undignified end for an astonishing periodical.

The Argus's principal coverage was of the six league teams in the Birmingham area: The Blues, Villa, Albion, Wolves, Walsall and, always rather oddly, Coventry. That doesn't tell one hundredth of the story. Results, and even brief reports, from the lower tiers of local football found their way into the paper and the middle pages did 'features' including jolly, comical caricatures of local players and managers. The first edition must have gone to print at about 4.50pm and although this opened up all kinds of possibilities for egregious inaccuracies – as tales that follow will illustrate – the one thing *The Argus* did with unerring precision was get the classified results right. Such attention was probably driven by the need to ensure that people could check their football pools coupon (look it up if you don't know). What was not included until the later editions, however, was an updated league table as this would, no doubt, have required a larger abacus than the one available in the *Argus* office.

The headlines would be broadly correct: ***Blues, Villa and Saddlers all held. Albion win. Wolves and Cov fall to defeat***. The match reports were a different story, particularly in the earlier editions. The copy probably needed to be ready by about 4.35pm and so it would have been common to read a report that had all the hallmarks of slanted local journalism and for this to take up the majority of the column inches allocated to that game. *Blues created chance after chance with a series of flowing moves* (like I said, local journalism) *and it was surprising that their visitors didn't concede again after the early goal. Vincent was terrorising opposition defenders and the Blues ace twice hit the woodwork …* you've got the picture. Wherever the journalist was happily sitting, he (and it would have been a he) could indulge in some leisurely cliché bashing to fill his copy and bang it over the wire before dropping in to The George for a couple on the way home. He lived in a world where whatever happened past 4.35pm would be allocated one sentence in the early edition. *With minutes to go, Millwall snatched an equaliser and then went upfield and scored again and so the Blues left the game empty-handed.* And that was how *The Argus* would deal with a dramatic finish: bare facts, one sentence, job done. In case you're wondering, the illustration used (it's not verbatim) is from Blues vs Millwall in September 1967. It's etched in the memory.

While *The Argus* served a purpose if you lived locally, some patchy radio coverage managed to provide some fairly rudimentary information if you were elsewhere. Holidays, however, were troublesome. Given that my entire working life has revolved around the school year, I have always taken my summer holiday in August – just as the season starts. This required making international phone calls at exorbitant prices. I do remember thinking in August 1998 that after phoning from a motel in deepest Montana at 10.30 in the morning to find out how we'd got on in our opening game against Port Vale away (won, 2-0) that I needed to have a word with myself. That conversation hasn't really taken place yet.

Although watching live diminished for me from the mid-70s and through the next decade, one thing remained, and remains still, unchanged. Whenever and wherever Blues are playing, barring genuine tragedy or mishap, I think of little else during that time and do not fully relax until I know the result. I have been lucky enough to have travelled the world, I am a grandfather, I have led a full and responsible professional life and have one undergraduate and two postgraduate degrees. I give this information not to be boastful but to offer a conundrum that I am still a long way from solving: given all of this, why do the perennially flagging fortunes of the club with which I formed a childhood affiliation persist to this extent? Why, in other words, am I obsessed? If you're still reading this and you're a supporter yourself, you're probably asking yourself the same thing. About yourself.

One thing's for certain. If football in the 1980s didn't suffocate the life out of this zeal, nothing ever could.

Chapter 4

Football becomes genuinely tragic

I'LL GET it out of the way from the start and then those of you of differing political persuasions can either stop reading and come back in three paragraphs' time or gloss over it and carry on: Thatcher hated football in the same way she hated working-class people. The political and social upheavals of the country during her decade in office were reflected in how football was organised, financed and, most specifically, supported. To attend a game, particularly in the Premier League, in 2020 is a world away from doing so in any division below the Championship; but it is not even in the same galaxy as the same event in the 1980s. Telling the same sort of middle-class people who now just love the footie that you attended games regularly during that era identified yourself as a real oddity. Hooliganism, recession, tragedy and stadia that hadn't moved on from the piss and meat smell I first encountered in the 1960s accounted for much of this.

The urban riots of the 80s and the miners' strike of 1984/85 all contributed to Thatcher's view of there being an 'enemy within' that had to be quelled. Her preferred method of doing so was the development of an increasingly militarised police force which enjoyed wages and working benefits unimaginable to those in the communities they were ostensibly serving. The same South Yorkshire force that had previously charged into unarmed strikers at Orgreave in 1984 were emboldened enough to treat working people with similar contempt at Hillsborough in 1989. 1985 saw death and disaster at the European Cup Final at the Heysel Stadium in Brussels involving Liverpool fans – 39 people died – as well as fire at Bradford's Valley Parade which killed 56. At Valley Parade an accumulation of rubbish under a wooden stand is believed to have been the cause, although the author Martin Fletcher still challenges this notion with the suggestion that it may have been a planned arson attack. Whatever the truth, the experience of crumbling stadia and aggressive policing characterised how football was experienced by crowds in the 80s. This mirrored the way in which a deliberately eviscerated manufacturing industry and political contempt for working-class people – 'there is no such thing as society' Thatcher intoned – characterised society as a whole in the 1980s.

On the same day as the Bradford fire, a 14-year-old boy was killed in rioting at St Andrew's where Blues were playing Leeds. It should have been a celebratory occasion as Blues went into the game, played in the Second Division, with promotion back to the First Division assured before the match had even started. Video footage exists of how events unfolded and there is no sugaring the pill: this was just dangerous, foolhardy behaviour on the part of hundreds, not dozens, of fans. One of Thatcher's acolytes, the pompous, self-satisfied 'businessman' David Evans, was in the throes of attempting to introduce a compulsory ID/membership scheme at Luton Town where he was chairman; his whinings would have been music to her ears. All of this was proof positive that football fans were to be despised and punished. As an illuminating coda to this, and to reinforce the idea that football was beyond the pale for people in the 1980s, it is interesting to note local commentary on Evans's death in 2008 describing him as 'loathsome' and a man despised 'by those of us who watched football before it was fashionable to do so'.

All of which is to establish that the backdrop to English football in the 1980s was grim. For Blues, it was even more so. So, before we go into detail, here's the record. In 1979 as the golden era of Francis, Latchford, Hatton, Burns, Kendall and the penguin shirt came to an end, we were relegated. But were immediately promoted the year after and remained in the First Division for four years. Then we were relegated again in 1984. And then we came up again the very next year. And then relegated the year after, remaining in the Second Division for the next three years before moving once again. Down to the Third Division in 1989. Ten years, two promotions, four relegations. Heady stuff, even by Blues' own high standards.

On top of all of this, the decade could not have started more inauspiciously for any Blues fan because in May 1981 Aston Villa became champions of England. They pipped Ipswich Town for the title with the Arsenal in third and our other neighbours, the Albion, in fourth. We had finished what was, by our own standards, a very respectable 11th which in any other season would have been something to crow about. There was no crowing in 1981, believe me. And if further proof were needed of the fact that these times could not have been more different, the Villa used 14 players in total in a 42-game season. Seven of those players played in every game. They made eight substitutions all season. It was a triumph that will never come close to being repeated. There. I've said it. I've given them their due.

Except that things got worse. The Villa qualified for the European Cup, which was a very different beast from the current, bloated Champions League. Ties were played on a home-and-away knockout basis and, oddly, to qualify you had to be the champions of your country. We watched through our fingers as they overcame some pretty big names – Dynamo Kiev, Anderlecht – to see them through to the final in Rotterdam in May 1982 where they were to play the mighty Bayern Munich, crammed to the rafters with World Cup winners and superstars. What, as they say, could possibly go wrong?

They won 1-0 and the goal, a stumbled tap-in, was scored by Peter Withe. Withe was a bundling, hustling centre-forward of the sort beloved by football fans throughout the ages. His early career was spent lumbering around lower leagues until, in 1975/76, he enjoyed an almost full season with … Birmingham City, for whom he scored nine goals in 35 appearances. If you visit Villa Park you will see, inscribed around the hoardings on the stands, the commentary of Withe's goal against Bayern. He stayed five seasons at the Villa, scoring 74 goals in 182 appearances and, in the process, justifying true legend status. Just to rub it in, he came back to the Blues for a loan period of eight games in 1987, scoring twice, before moving off to finish his career in undistinguished style at Huddersfield Town. It really is very Birmingham City to have had on our books a player who embodied mediocrity in our shirt and who saved his heroics for others – and in this case, the worst sort of others as far as we were concerned.

There was a glimmer of light in all of this. Well, it was more like a bash of thunder and lightning of a magnesium-flash pyrotechnic order. At the start of the 1982 season, Aston Villa were, indeed, champions of Europe. Our first meeting with these international conquerors was to be on 27 December 1982 at St

Andrew's. Two days after Christmas and seven days after I got married. I wasn't going to miss this and in an act of selfless devotion that has characterised the marriage that has lasted since, I arranged a sort of honeymoon that managed to take us past the Blues ground on that day of days.

The previous chapter tells of our cup runs in the late 60s and 70s when crowds of 50 and 60,000 crammed unfeasibly into St Andrew's. The impending football malaise that shrouded miserably around much of the country, and the blue half of Birmingham in particular, was reflected in the 1982/83 season in measly crowds of between 12 and 14,000. At the end of the season, when Blues pulled off one of their more spectacular escapes by winning five and drawing one of our last six games, four of those games were at home and the average attendance was 13,800. So when 43,864 people turned up just after Christmas 1982, including my new bride and myself, this was something special in the days when people had fallen out of love with the game.

What happened rings the bells nearly 40 years on. A 3-0 win in the sort of game that simply doesn't happen any more – where it was accepted by all parties that usual rules about physical contact, retaliation and retribution were to be more honoured in the breach than the observance. In those days all teams knew how to 'take care of themselves' but it does have to be said that the Birmingham City side of that era were probably better equipped than most to do so. The core of this platoon of men, the footballing spine – that is from goalkeeper through to centre-half to centre-forward – comprised Tony Coton, Noel Blake and Mick Harford. They are all still very intimidating physical specimens and they took this muscularity into games with great gusto along with, according to both recorded fact and exaggerated legend, the issue that they were all somewhere on the scale from permanently angry to occasionally deranged.

Other books, including biographies of and by players themselves, have documented the reputation of many of the Birmingham players of that era. Similarly, there is no shortage of the chronicles of the Zulu Army and its own mix of bravery, anti-racism and occasionally anarchistic behaviour. I have sometimes enjoyed witnessing the latter and at other times been appalled by it. I never observed the fabled drinking and aggression of some of the players during the 80s, although to judge by the number of people who swear they did, those very players must have been on the razz 24/7. I have little doubt that there is significant substance behind some of the mythology. I'm making no judgement because that is not what this book is about, but one thing is undeniable. There has been since that era, and there remains still, a sort of rebellious lairyness about the Blues and some of our supporters. At St Andrew's on 27 December 1982, it was there in bucketloads. The place just seemed quite mad. The fact that Noel Blake, the epitome of the hardman that many Blues fans themselves wanted to be, was on the scoresheet made the whole event even more ridiculously enjoyable.

The 43,864 all seemed to make their way home quite peaceably as far as I can remember, although I may have been too stupefied to notice. It's just as well that I did manage to enjoy that moment of rare euphoria. As far as my affiliation to Birmingham City was concerned, that was just about it for the best part of a decade.

The remarkable run at the end of the 1982/83 season referred to above marked a temporary lifting of the clouds, but we were relegated again in May 1984. A year later we were promoted in a season during which my own opportunities for watching became ever more limited – a circumstance mirroring the ever-plummeting unpopularity of football as a spectator sport. In a promotion year, crowds at St Andrew's rarely exceeded 12,000. Our only local rivals in the Second Division that season were Wolves, for whom only 10,236 turned up. In the month prior to promotion and the fateful Leeds game, two consecutive home games against Palace and Charlton attracted two attendances that just scraped above 10,000. On a further personal note – and I'm afraid there are one or two more to come – my stepfather, who had been going to games all his life and who watched from the safety and security of the placid and largely aged Main Stand, gave up the ghost, having been knocked to the ground by an errant police horse outside the ground. It was a shocking last straw for a man typical of his generation of football supporters for whom going to the match was becoming an increasingly depressing and disconcerting experience.

There are seasons that all supporters would like to forget; that's a given. But then there was 1985/86. By now we were in the era of three points for a win. And we started well enough. A home win on the opening day of the season against West Ham – watched by 11,164 – was followed by a couple of defeats at Watford and Chelsea, but then a decent run saw us with 16 points after nine games and on 21 September we were eighth in the league table. We knew – and I mean *knew* – it was too good to be true, but even for those of us inured to impending doom and failure, what happened next was ridiculously spectacular. We lost the next eight games after 21 September, scoring two goals in the process. We then managed a goalless draw at the Arsenal at the end of November, before losing four more on the bounce. By that time, we had slid to 21st in a 22-team league (we'll come to the only smidgeon of mirth to be had from this in due course) – a position from which we did not move all season. We finished the season with seven more defeats on the bounce, meaning that in 33 games we had secured 13 points, scoring 20 goals, four of them in a 4-4 draw with Coventry. The only two bits of merriment in all of this came first from our neighbours at the Albion, who were even worse. They had managed a mere 24 points to our 29, winning on four occasions throughout the season – although in a savage twist, twice against us. In our last 12 games of the season, we lost ten times, drew once, at home to Manchester United, and won once away. At Villa Park.

It is a measure of how desperately awful 1986 was that even this most remarkable and unexpected of victories – 3-0 – could be considered to be a waste. We could have done with it on so many other occasions that to use it up when we were so firmly anchored in 21st place is infuriating. Almost all supporters that I know happily take up the 'only at my club' position. Only at my club could we sell our star striker for eightpence and install the cleaner as manager – you know the sort of thing. But, really. Really. Only at my club could we save one of our three wins in seven months for a hugely enjoyable but ultimately meaningless victory over the neighbours. As well as getting knocked out of the cup by a non-league team.

Yep. That too. Our third-round FA Cup tie against non-league Altrincham was postponed because of snow and ice on 11 January and was played on the evening of Tuesday, 14 January. Birmingham City 1, Altrincham 2. Attendance: 6,636.

My son was born a few hours afterwards on 15 January and so I'd like to say I didn't care about the result. To my shame, I did, but it was somewhat eclipsed and the birth did save me from some of the regulation ribbing that should have come my way. One football supporting friend, however, did not let me off so lightly, even though there has been a beneficial and enduring legacy from his actions. It had been his practice to buy the newspaper for friends on the days of their children's births and so I was very pleased to receive this gift from him; *The Guardian* newspaper of 15 January 1986. With it came a brief note: 'you may have a good deal of fun explaining events on the front page to your son but those on the back will set you a greater challenge'.

The front-page story to which he was referring was the Westland helicopter crisis which had reached its peak that same day. Westland was the last British firm to make helicopters and, in common with so much manufacturing in Britain, was in a desperate state. It was the subject of two potential rescue bids, one from European firms and one from an American. Thatcher herself favoured the Americans, her Defence Secretary, Michael Heseltine, the Europeans. (Is this all sounding a touch familiar, by the way?) Thatcher, as ever, was insistent that her way was the only choice and Heseltine resigned, threatening to split the Tory Cabinet and imperil Thatcher's supremacy at the same time. Although things rested on a knife edge, she survived and went on to do another few years' worth of damage. I honestly can't recall if I have ever discussed this political episode with my son, but I do know that along with football's general demise it did at least manage to deflect attention from an FA Cup humiliation witnessed live by 6,000 people rattling around in a freezing St Andrew's on a Tuesday night.

As for the back page, I am afraid that in a series of actions that amount to a cross between child abuse and persistent but subtle indoctrination, the only riposte is to say that he found out the hard way. My southern-born son did grow up to love sport and to share his father's obsession with football and cricket. I scrupulously laid out the ground rules for who he might wish to support – honest, M'lud – and although there was some dabbling here and there on his part along the way and, indeed, excursions to grounds all and sundry across the nation, he settled on the fact that he was, indeed, a Birmingham City supporter. The point at which this happened was after the appointment of Barry Fry in 1993 about which, inevitably, there will be more in a later chapter. Perhaps the point at which he made his final decision was in January 1994 when, in a reprise of the events on the night prior to his birth, we lost at home in the third round of the FA Cup to non-league Kidderminster Harriers. He must have sensed that we were, well, different. And so there he was/is: scarred for life by a careless father. We're keeping a very close eye on his own son.

After Altrincham there followed three seasons so utterly dismal that even a non-Blues fan would be reaching for the razors and paracetamol. I'll keep it brief. Following relegation in 1986, there was temporary, deluded talk of an immediate return. This was enflamed by a return of seven points from our first three games and that was just about it for the season. Home attendances hovered between seven and nine thousand and in the final 15 games of the season, a paltry 11 points were acquired. When the Blues played Grimsby, who were already relegated, on 2 May 1987, 4,457 people turned up. Earlier in the season, our FA Cup incompetence was further enhanced by losing to neighbours Walsall. As it happens, this was to be nothing more than a harbinger of our complete nadir when, two seasons later, they defeated us 5-0 on our way to the Third Division. The intervening 1987/88 season followed much the same pattern, with the tedium leavened only by another victory at Villa Park very early in the season. As with the fateful final day in 1985, the final game of the season was at home to Leeds. This time a mere 6,024 witnessed a goalless draw. Better, of course, a dull meaningless game watched only by the desperately addicted than riot and manslaughter. All the same, the death rattle for football seemed to gurgle ever louder.

In May 1989 we were finally, almost mercifully, relegated to the third tier of English football, where we remained for four of the next six years – up in 92, down in 94, up in 95. So ended one of the most miserable and depressing decades of the club's history. But before we leave it, we must turn to those responsible. During that period, in common with a great many football clubs at the time, we were owned by the greedy and the unscrupulous and managed by a combination of the willing, the desperate and the disillusioned. When it came to managers, nobody – but nobody – epitomised the miserabilism of the 1980s more than Ron Saunders.

Saunders was clearly cut from a different cloth from other men. It was he who had guided the neighbours to the league triumph in 1981. He was a stickler for fitness and discipline and he was a man to whom a joke was akin to blasphemy. A famous photograph of him training with his Norwich team in 1972 shows him running, Putin-like, bare-chested and muscle-bound, while his protégés gaze on admiringly. And what's more, Ron Saunders can still win you money in a pub bet. 'Who was Villa's manager when they won the European Cup in 1982?' you can ask and the answer will almost certainly come back – 'Ron Saunders' – and you can pick up your winnings. Because on 9 February 1982 Ron Saunders had a row with the board of Aston Villa and a few weeks later took up his next position ... at Birmingham City. (Tony Barton, just in case you're interested.) Why d'ya do it, Ron? Why? The only answer must lie in the existence of some sort of fates that dictate that during the most wretched and dreary of times in the history of Birmingham City Football Club, the gods decreed that we should have bestowed upon us a manager to fit the mood. Saunders presided over a 16th- and then a 17th-place finish before relegation in 1984. He saw us to an immediate return in 1985 before the woeful 1985/86 Altrincham game and the ensuing relegation. He was sacked the day after the Altrincham fiasco and then moved on to take the job at the Albion who were even worse than us and were relegated with 24 points in a 42-game season. In September 1987 the Albion gave him the sack and that was his last managerial job. I'd like to think he spent his retirement years working as a children's entertainer or leading community singing in an old-persons' home. There had to be some happiness in his life and perhaps our neighbours had seen the best of him: he is etched into the history of BCFC as a melancholy man mirroring the downtrodden nature of the team he managed and those who supported it.

Goodness only knows what it was like behind the scenes at St Andrew's in the 1980s. One thing is beyond dispute. With crowds of four figures – and we're talking low four figures – and in an era well before big TV money (who'd have watched us, anyway?) or major advertising and sponsorship deals, there would have been zero money. I'm aware of the fact that football journalism is now littered with financial experts and that the big four accountancy firms have football specialists at their disposal, but I still firmly subscribe to the frustrated terrace chant of 'where's the money gone?' when it comes to football finances. In the last decade or so, the answer to that at the top level is easy – into the pockets of the players themselves. In the 80s the money from the sales of Trevor, Kenny Burns and

Bob Latchford obviously disappeared into the sort of financial void that football so readily creates for itself. Given the sort of people in charge, that hardly comes as a shock.

In the early 1950s Len Shackleton was a tricky forward who played most of his career at Sunderland and won five caps for England. He had a reputation as something of a joker and his 1956 autobiography was entitled *The Clown Prince of Soccer*. In it was included one of the most famous chapters written about football. Under the title of 'The average director's knowledge of football' there appeared a blank page. In modern times, when the camera pans in on some visiting foreign dignity dropping by to look at his latest investment, accompanied by a lavishly wrapped trophy wife who is plainly bored to the point of fever, it's easy to bring Shackleton's view to mind.

In the 1980s – and Blues weren't alone in this in the same way that they are not at present – clubs were run by small(minded) businessmen who brought to British football all the acumen, skill and foresight that they did to British industry as a whole. At the helm at Birmingham City was local scrap dealer, Ken Wheldon. His former footballing allegiance was with Walsall, a club about which it is worth a few sentences of digression.

I can't speak with any certainty for fans of our other neighbours, but I suspect that what holds true for Blues fans about Walsall does for them as well. From the start of the 1970s, Blues, Villa and the Albion all had spells in the third tier of English football and Wolves managed to slide even lower into the fourth in 1986/87. Although Walsall managed the very occasional holiday in the second tier, they habitually resided in the third and fourth tiers, nestled in the oft-renamed Fellows Park in the bucolic and restful setting of the newly constructed M6 motorway. Players from the 'bigger' local clubs often chose to finish their careers there and there was, and remains, a genuine affection for a non-threatening, plucky country cousin. As far as Blues were concerned, this cosy relationship became a little more strained as our actual meetings in the lower leagues became all too frequent: the 5-0 thrashing on our way down in 1989 (representing, incidentally, 12 per cent of Walsall's total goalscoring that season) finally demonstrating that any innate sense of superiority was stupidly misplaced. For all of that, Blues fans generally have a soft spot for the Saddlers.

Wheldon severed his connection with Walsall, bought Birmingham City for 25p (allegedly – I can find no proof that this unlikely transaction was quite so cheap) inheriting £3 million worth of liabilities along the way. Research reveals little of Wheldon, his life and his dealings and so other than the evident running down of all assets belonging to Birmingham City, including the selling off of training facilities and an obvious neglect of a crumbling stadium, details are scant. The 80s was a time of genuine recession and mass unemployment – both factors which contributed to declining match attendances. Along with this was a culture of reckless acquisition just so long as profit, any kind of profit and at whatever human cost, could be achieved. By the time Wheldon sold the club to Ramesh, Bimal and Samesh Kumar in 1989, he had reduced the deficit to £500,000, so by the standards of the day he had done well. The effect on his personal wealth is not recorded but, frankly, it's difficult to see how he could have made any money. He just held an asset against which he could borrow. As events at the time of writing in 2020 have proved, a football club that you don't care about is still handy to have in your financial portfolio.

Wheldon sold up in 1989 with the Kumar brothers taking over. If the Kumars did actually have any real money it disappeared, allegedly, with the collapse of the Bank of Credit and Commerce International (BCCI) in 1991. Their investment and interest in Birmingham City occasionally prompted speculative stories about plans and developments, none of which ever materialised. During that period, my own attendance at St Andrew's and at away games was only ever intermittent, but the only thing I can positively say about the Kumars' tenure is that in all of the criticism and anger directed against them, I never heard a racist slur used, which is not to say that racist language and behaviour was rare. That was not the case then and, although comparatively rare, it is not the case now. It is instructive that once again in times of social and economic uncertainty that vile racist behaviour and language has resurfaced in football, aided and abetted by the handy, careless instrument of social media. To borrow from Nick Hornby when talking about racism in football, it comes to something when you're happy to hear your owners called just plain old 'bastards' and not 'Paki bastards'.

The 70s had been almost good: reflected in the light of the 80s, they were halcyon days. We'd enjoyed the benign, avuncular management style of Freddie Goodwin and Jim Smith. We'd even had World Cup winner Sir Alf Ramsey in charge for a few months in 1977 and 78. The Coombs family seemed to run the club at arm's length and we enjoyed the best part of a decade in the top flight doing perfectly OK with some wonderful players. The departure of Jim Smith heralded the 80s and the age of Saunders, Wheldon and the era of the 6,000 crowd – albeit that such meagre attendances had their roots in circumstances beyond the control of these individuals. From Saunders to John Bond, to Dave Mackay, to Lou Macari to Terry Cooper, with a brief interregnum for local hero, but bemused manager, Gary Pendrey, a succession of former bigwigs and ex-internationals inflicted on us brief snaps of humiliating failure. There was yet to be more frustration and disappointment but, as someone famously said as the end of the next decade approached, things could only get better.

Note: In the early days of December 2019, the deaths were announced of both Ron Saunders and Jim Smith, the former at 87, the latter at 79. The demise of both of these stalwarts prompted much reflection about a footballing age that is long past and the usual speculation about how they would have got along with the rather more delicate version of the game of whose history, particularly in the Birmingham area, they both formed a central part. From a Blues point of view, it is unsurprising that Smith is remembered with more affection than Saunders. Forced to sell Trevor, Smith compensated by putting together a team of genuine character. It was crammed with personalities from Archie Gemmill to Alan Curbishley to the extraordinary Frank Worthington and bolstered by the presence of the excellent Keith Bertschin up front. On the last day of the 1980 season, in front of a bellowing 33,863 at St Andrew's, this wonderful team did its level best to mess up automatic promotion in a nerve-wrenching 3-3 draw with Notts County, but eventually prevailed to pip Chelsea into the third place that guaranteed going up at that time. The tributes bestowed upon Smith all talk of a man of great humour and humanity – and that's certainly how he came across to all of us.

None of which is to downplay the astonishing achievements of Ron Saunders, albeit that his accomplishments were of benefit almost exclusively to our chums over in Aston. A few days before his death, the demise was announced of England fast bowler and captain, Bob Willis, who also had strong Birmingham connections but never really captured the hearts of his adopted public there. All of which goes to show that you don't have to like your heroes and that it's stupid to project personality traits on to your chosen villains – which, I admit, I may have done to Ron Saunders earlier in this chapter. So, rest in peace, boys – you're all part of our history.

Chapter 5

The Barry Frydays. Barminess prevails, quite often in a good way

IN 1990 everyone remembered that football was a good thing. The BBC had the urbane Des Lynam schmoozing his way through their coverage of the World Cup which, in a precursor of the uber-marketing that was to infect football, was branded as *Italia 90*. England got to the semi-final and Gary Lineker not only scored lots of very good goals but also emerged as quite a sensible and articulate human being – qualities which have since earned him approval and opprobrium in equal measure, the latter especially the case in the age of the keyboard activist. The marketability of this 'product' that was so besmirched and derided in the previous decade did not go unnoticed. There was money to be made and many went to it with a will.

Hillsborough in 1989 had seen football stumble to the bottom of the pit. The heroic campaigning of the victims' families has set the record straight but at the time, the prevailing discourse was one of hooligan elements bringing about their own downfall and reaping what they had sown. This point of view was wickedly amplified by *The Sun* newspaper whose owners still seem unmoved and unworried by their own scandalous behaviour. Attendances at matches continued to tumble and even the occasional midweek glance at the glamour of European football was denied as English clubs underwent a five-year ban following the horror of Heysel in 1985.

As far as the Blues were concerned, 1989 took some beating for wretchedness. The season started with three points gleaned from the first eight games. The eighth of these took place at home to Plymouth Argyle in front of 4,435 people and plonked us firmly into 24th place, which we occupied for the majority of the season. Relegation duly ensued in May 1989 and only the greater ineptitude of our pals in Walsall saved us from bottom place. We scored 31 goals in 46 games and conceded 76 in acquiring 35 points. On a personal level, the only saving grace was that I didn't have to watch them for most of the season as other events in my life took precedence.

The season ended with an away defeat at Crystal Palace where Blues took huge numbers of fans. Some estimates put it at 9,000, which is odd when you look at the pitiful home attendances for that season. An elaborate and well-observed fancy dress code promised to make the day a jolly one at least. Relegation was well and truly assured and even though Palace had an outside chance of automatic promotion, this depended on a set of convoluted outcomes both at Selhurst Park and elsewhere. As it happens, even though they were eventually promoted, it was through the play-offs and not as a result of that final day.

The day was far from jolly. I'm sure some battle-hardened Zulu will take issue with me about this because the day has gone down in the collective consciousness of some as one of the great away trips. It wasn't. In the shadow of Hillsborough some five weeks earlier, many of the 9,000 behaved with a degree of irresponsibility that was jaw-droppingly stupid. The fact that they may have been attired as nuns, sharks or Hitler scarcely diminishes the level of foolishness and unwarranted aggression on show. In the six home games prior to the Palace fixture, the average attendance was 4,800; those at Selhurst weren't the dyed-in-the-wool contingent. The fact that there were no casualties, and the fact that this even has to be mentioned, gives a flavour of the times. Grim and belligerent.

Into this strode Des and Gary and Gazza and Pavorotti singing 'Nessun Dorma'. Within two years we had the Premier League and Sky TV and football knew that it could reach out to a different, more affluent audience. Soon we had all-seater stadia at the top end of the game, some of which have now evolved into futuristic pleasure domes catering to man's every consumable need. And I acknowledge some of the contradictions that bedevil my views about this enduring sea change in how the game is presented and marketed. Do I want numpties climbing on floodlights and urinating on the people below? Unsurprisingly not. Do I want children to be able to attend live games without being frightened? Yep. Do I enjoy the possibility of seeing football regularly on TV? Broadly speaking, and with some reservations about overkill, yes.

But do I want an opposition player to be nervous about taking a corner in front of a hissing, bubbling Tilton? I certainly do. Do I take pride in hearing opposition fans say that they find (or, as of recent times, found) St Andrew's intimidating? You bet. Do I regret witnessing the gradual, and now almost complete, elimination of hefty physical challenges in the game and the uproarious effect that it has on crowds? Absolutely. I want, like many fans, the best of both worlds – but without the threat of the urine splash.

So down we went in 1989 and finished seventh in the third tier in 1990 and 12th in 1991. But in 1991 we went, at last, to Wembley. And won.

One of the few consolations to be gained from sloshing around in the lower levels of English football is entry into the cup designated for teams at that level. Such competitions have been sponsored by varying businesses over the years. In 1991 it was Leyland

Daf. The competition was positively Byzantine in its structure: it started on 6 November 1990 and finished on 26 May 1991. There were group stages, northern and southern sections and two-legged semi-finals. All of which resulted in 58,756 people turning up at Wembley to watch Blues play Tranmere Rovers in the final. Of those present, the estimate was that some 40,000 were Blues fans. As with all such appearances for so many clubs at HA9 0WS, the question about where they had been for the rest of the season fails to go away.

There is extensive footage of the final which will always be remembered for two goals by John Gayle. Gayle was a lump but was relatively local and we all liked him. The first of his goals came from a swift turn to glide past a defender followed by a crisp, unstoppable shot. The justifiably discredited Ron Atkinson was commentating and was moved to observe that he 'didn't think he possessed that sort of skill'. It was a sentiment echoed by many of us celebrating in the stands but, as it turned out, it was nothing more than a taster for an even more delicious and unlikely main course.

Having gone two goals up, it appeared that we were going to leave Wembley with a trophy of sorts and we were all happy enough with that. However, in true Blues style, the two-goal lead disappeared and at 2-2 failure and disappointment seemed inevitable. And then Gayle scored a goal that put his excellent first effort into the shade. In an earlier chapter I attempted to describe Barry Bridges's miracle against the Arsenal in 1968 of which there is no photographic or filmed record. Gayle's second in the Leyland Daf Final 23 years later does not suffer the same fate.

Like I said, John Gayle was a big man. I'm not sure how he'd have got on in the days of bleep tests, clean living and regulated diets but that probably applied to most of his contemporaries. For all of this, he exhibited a moment of unparalleled grace, athleticism and skill that is there for all to see. A long free kick is pumped into the opposition area, another lump, Vince Overson, heads it onwards and then Gayle twists to execute an overhead kick that spears, unstoppably, into the goal. 'I don't know what he's been taking lately,' blurts careless Ron Atkinson, 'but this isn't the Gayle I've known over the years.' In 44 games for Blues, Gayle scored ten goals, so that was eight more in 42 games which is a mediocre record that is entirely inconsequential. If he's still being bought drinks on the back of that one glorious moment, he deserves them.

We went back to Wembley in 1995 and repeated the feat but, my goodness, plenty happened in between.

In 1992 we were promoted back to the second tier under the sensible management of former England international, Terry Cooper. Home crowds gradually improved along with football's new-found social acceptability and we could have even convinced ourselves that things really did have a chance of getting better. This illusion was given some credibility when we won the first four games of the season, which was just as well, as we managed just one victory after that until the turn of the new year. From there ensued the usual bumping around in the relegation zone but even by our own very, very high standards, one particular piece of self-immolation stands out as we approached the end of the season. Easter Monday 1993 has a special place in our hearts.

Swindon Town had sidled into the consciousness of the football world by employing former international star Glenn Hoddle as their player-manager. They were fourth in the table with an outside chance of promotion; we were 18th out of 24 and still in need of at least a couple of wins to be assured of safety. In front of a decent bank holiday St Andrew's crowd of 17,903 we set to it with a will and with 30 minutes remaining we led 4-1. Three precious points almost in the bag.

There is any number of reasons why I try not to leave games early and the events of 12 April 1993 furnish convincing justification for this. Final score: Birmingham City 4, Swindon Town 6. No misprint here, dear reader; you got it right. Three goals up at home in an important game and we ship five in half an hour. Things like that inflict lasting, scarring damage on a person. Two draws in the next four games along with two defeats meant another last-day battle for survival – and there'd be plenty more of those in the next quarter of a century – in which a 1-0 win at home to Charlton meant that we stayed up. Oddly, no one much remembers that game; the Swindon debacle had, perhaps, dulled our senses. But if it had done, what was to follow certainly had the effect of jolting them to life.

By now BCCI had gone bust and with it went the Kumars and their questionable financial contribution to the wealth and development of Birmingham City. The minutiae of receivership and liquidators became part of the language of football supporters and although our jaunt to Wembley and a decent promotion season in 1992 created the illusion of things bowling along nicely, a crumbling stadium and a growing reputation for institutional ineptitude always ensured an air of fatality around the club. The last-day survival of 1993 was only a forestalling of the inevitable and the start of the new season unfolded to confirm our worst fears. Six straight defeats from the start of November plonked us in our familiar position near the bottom of the table and then something – well quite a big thing – happened.

People who peddled soft pornography bought Birmingham City. The Gold brothers, David and Ralph, joined forces with David Sullivan and the entrepreneur and businesswoman, Karren Brady. This was kind of glamorous, particularly for a club previously owned by local traders, scrap metal merchants and cut-price drapers. The wealth gleaned from the selling of an idea of sex was now going to prop up a club in the heart of a city whose diminishing wealth was rooted in a tougher, harder and much less glamorous view of the world. Forgive the profanity, but there was a strong view that we'd been fucked over by enough charlatans in the past not to be too coy about grabbing the money from those for whom the encouragement of fucking was their core business.

If our new owners enjoyed a patina of the naughty along with the glamorous, the choice of manager to replace dear old, worn-out Terry Cooper, was just plain bizarre. Barry Francis Fry had bumbled through the most undistinguished of playing careers despite beginning as an apprentice with Manchester United. His longest spell in 12 years of knocking around the fringes of the semi-pro world was a 50-game spell with Romford, for whom he scored eight goals. His managerial career started at a similar sort of level before he settled into a long spell at Barnet, where he was sacked and reinstated on eight, yes eight, separate occasions by chairman, Stan Flashman – whose own interesting career would merit a volume of its own. Having left Barnet to manage Southend, Fry had one season there where he managed to save them from relegation and on the back of this, for reasons that can only be guessed at, our purveyors of sex toys and lingerie decided that he was the man for Birmingham City.

Fry was quite mad. As such, many people – myself included – thought he was the perfect fit for us. When he took up his position in December 1993, Blues were in 20th place in the First Division (the second tier) having lost six times in a row. There was a 'new manager bounce' and we won our first game – at home to Charlton – on 18 December. Defeat away to Stoke on Boxing Day followed, but two days later, in front of 28,228 people at St Andrew's, we beat the Albion. We were definitely on the up. This Fry bloke wasn't just some old joker from the Fens – he knew what he was doing.

We didn't win again for another 14 league games and along the way, in homage to the Altrincham debacle eight years earlier, we lost at home to non-league Kidderminster in the third round of the FA Cup. So he was, indeed, just some old joker from the Fens and the owners had dropped a clanger of ear-splitting proportions.

In a rather charming aside, despite this making for very grim viewing for the new ownership team, one of them had clearly spotted something of great attraction. Two years after the takeover, Karren Brady married the Blues striker, Paul Peschisolido. One of Fry's prime characteristics, and the one for which he is remembered with a mixture of head-shaking bemusement and great merriment, was his fondness for buying and selling players. He did so at breakneck speed, without the slightest evidence of any strategy whatsoever and with no apparent regard for either the ability of the player involved or where he might fit into any kind of plan. Nobody could say with any confidence, therefore, why Peschisolido was sold to Stoke at the end of the season or who prompted the move – Brady or Fry or the tooth fairy. But off he went, having scored 17 goals in 43 games for us … only to return some 18 months later to play nine more games before being sold to the Albion. This toing and froing became entirely commonplace during Fry's tenure.

His first season ended in failure … just. After the Easter period, Blues were rooted in 23rd place with seven games left. The owners had held true to an initial promise to rebuild parts of the ground and the work was to start in April. This meant that these fixtures had to be juggled around and the net outcome was that we were to play our last four games away from home. In one of the many ridiculous twists of fate and form to which, after nearly 30 years of watching, I had become entirely accustomed, we acquired 17 points from those seven games – five wins and two draws. We won three of the four away games, including a raucous, mad win, 4-2, down the road at the Albion – themselves in danger of relegation. On the final day of the season – here we were again – we needed to do better at Tranmere than the Albion down at Portsmouth. We won. So did the Albion. We went down. And so ended the first chapter of the Barry Fry era.

To their credit, the owners must have spotted something with which it was worthwhile persevering. Fry's antics and his conduct with the media weren't to the liking of all Blues fans. Many considered them as adding to the perception that we were becoming a bit of a circus. Fry's claim that he had lifted a gypsy curse on St Andrew's by piddling in each of the four corners was typical of his harmless, but slightly embarrassing, buffoonery. Others, and as I say, I veered towards this camp, embraced the anarchy and unpredictability that became the by-products of Fry's leadership. Triple substitutions became relatively commonplace and the acquisition of forward after forward, most of them unutterably hopeless, scarcely merited comment. In the course of Fry's second season, he used 38 players in 46 games. And, as it turned out, it was a very good season indeed.

St Andrew's had been renovated and it looked a good deal better, but on a personal level, a part of my history disappeared. Prior to the run of four away games at the end of the previous season, the last game before the rebuilding took place on 16 April, a day after my 41st birthday and some 31 years since my first acquaintance with the smoke, the steam, the meat smell and the piss. We played Bristol City and, in true Blues style, nearly messed up our last game at the old St Andrew's before escaping with a 2-2 draw. As can happen in April in England, the game was played in intermittent snow showers and sunshine. In the era before the internet allowed us to trace former friends and flames, imperilling many a marriage along the way, I was unsurprised to meet up with many of the old crew as we gravitated to our old spot from schoolboy days – including, in a touching way, one of the Villa-supporting fraternity who had come to pay his nostalgic respects. My current season ticket is located just a few rows away and, no, I still don't like sitting down at football.

But the rebuilt St Andrew's was an improvement and Fry, indulged by the porn merchants, traded with continuing abandon and in a way that took us to the top of the table and an instant return to the second tier. In a complete reversal of our usual fortunes, we also emerged with enormous credit from the third round of the FA Cup. Being in the Third Division meant that we had to suffer the indignity of playing in the earlier rounds, but we negotiated eventual victories against the might of Slough Town and Scunthorpe United and were rewarded with a home tie, in our sparkly new stadium, against the mighty Liverpool. Home attendances were levelling out at about 17,000 and so even though the heady days of the 50,000s were now part of a bygone era, a very respectable 25,326, just short of capacity, witnessed a creditable 0-0 draw, the highlights of which we could enjoy on national, terrestrial television, before the replay at Anfield. Where we were sure to get murdered.

Except that we didn't. Liverpool took the lead and this was supposed to herald the regulation home win that everyone expected. But we scored a goal through the flamboyant Ricky Otto, who wasn't really flamboyant at all but had dreadlocks and tried to dribble a lot and so that was good enough. Oh, and he had a violent past and a scar and was picked up courtesy of the police in Hackney during his time at Blues on suspicion of possessing cannabis. Yes. Black man stopped by police in East London for having the gall to own a decent car. After football, Otto became a probation officer and a committed Christian. He made his mark at Blues by scoring twice in a 1-1 draw on his debut (work it out) before scoring the winner at Cardiff two days later. His magnificent effort at Anfield came to naught as we went on to lose, spectacularly, on penalties, missing every one we took. But for a few glorious moments, Ricky put us in the spotlight and because of that, his subsequent mediocrity, along with that of a good many of Fry's purchases, fades in the memory.

What's more, we went to Wembley and won again. This year's sponsors were Auto Windscreens and the route to the final was marginally less convoluted than that in 1991. Our opponents were Carlisle United who, on the back of a peculiar kit sponsored by haulage firm Eddie Stobart, had dubbed themselves the 'deckchair army'. The final was the first to be decided by another new-fangled innovation, the golden goal. The footballing authorities (I use the term in the sense that they governed the game, not that they brought any genuine authority to that exercise) hoped that this device would have the effect of teams being more ambitious during turgid periods of extra time which ended with the unsatisfactory lottery of penalty shoot-outs. As it turned out, the opposite effect was achieved as teams became ever more cautious about making the one crucial error that would settle the game in a moment, with absolutely no chance of any kind of comeback. Indeed, when Paul Tait scored the goal that won the game for us in extra time, it took a few moments to realise that this was, in fact, the end of the game. But as every Blues fan knows, despite this novelty ensuring that we made national news, Paul Tait's goal will go down in our history for a very different reason.

Tait was a local boy and Blues supporter who made 170 of his 271 professional appearances for us. As he wheeled away after scoring at Wembley, he tore off his top to reveal a tee shirt resplendent with the slogan 'Shit on the Villa'. The words echo a favourite terrace refrain down the ages, sung to the tune of 'Roll out the Barrel'. It's not exactly Rodgers and Hammerstein but it's an enduring favourite and one that few other sets of supporters have requisitioned. Even when they do, it is rarely sung with the venom and hatred, incubated through the ages, that can be felt when sung at its most energetic. Occasionally, Villa fans try it by substituting 'City' for 'Villa'. It's a tragic and embarrassing mistake on their part for a number of reasons.

First, no one, but no one, refers to us as 'City'. No one has ever asked their mate if they're going down to watch City on Saturday, meaning the Blues. Second, and given that this is the case, why would you want to shit on the city of Birmingham – the place where your team and club are located? And thereby hangs the tale ... because a great many of you aren't from Birmingham at all, are you? Nuneaton, Lichfield, Stafford, Worcester and Sutton bloody Coldfield maybe. You're not proper Brummies at all so that's why you end up singing nonsense like 'Shit on the City'.

At least, so goes the accepted 'wisdom' among Blues fans. It's largely nonsensical but that's not the point. There is some truth that the Villa have always attracted support from a wider area than central Birmingham and its immediate suburbs but this rustic analysis serves the proper purpose of fuelling the rivalry and bitterness that the current guardians of the game are so keen to quell and anaesthetise. So when Paul Tait displayed his allegiance in this moment of drama – even though most of us couldn't possibly have read it from where we were in the ground – he had certainly judged the temperament and mindset of his intended audience. He was fined two weeks' wages for his antics but assuming he never had to buy a drink for himself – like John Gayle – for the next few years, that wouldn't have been too severe an imposition.

As it happens, Tait had to vie with quite a few of his team-mates for full hero status. Fry had certainly purchased some big characters, including the itinerant but free-scoring Steve Claridge and the bullish Liam Daish. However, the biggest – in terms of stature – came in the form of another Blues-supporting Birmingham boy when, in January 1995, Kevin Francis was bought from Stockport for £800,000.

It might be tempting to wander off into some metaphysical analysis along the lines of how this purchase, evoking the name of one of the few greats ever to wear the shirt, was a symbol of times lost. A quarter of a century earlier we had a Francis who epitomised grace, style, speed and future promise. He had gone on to play for his country over 50 times, scoring 12 goals, and had been courted by many of Europe's top sides. Now we had a lanky loon of a lad who had scored 88 goals in 152 games for Stockport County, whose career once he left Blues petered out in non-league obscurity. He did enjoy an international career of sorts, stepping out twice for St Kitts and Nevis but failing to trouble the scorers. All of which counted for nothing because we took him to our hearts and every one of the 13 goals he scored in his 73 appearances genuinely did seem to come from the soul of his Blues affiliation. I'm fully aware of the fact that I'm projecting sentiments here, but that was really how it seemed.

Four of those 13 goals were scored in the League Cup of 1995/96, three of which were up there with the greats. Two were against Middlesbrough, then in the Premier League and one, later in the competition, against high-flyers, Leeds United. All three are available to see online and share a commonality with John Gayle's efforts at Wembley in terms of the reaction they elicit from the TV commentators at the time. Put simply, all of them give due credit to wonderful goals before adding, in tones of clear bewilderment, that they really didn't think he had it in him. The first of the three in December 1995, on an ice-bound pitch flanked by piled snow, is a thing of comic genius.

The bony frame of Kevin Francis was ill-suited to the skating rink on which the game was played. In fairness, many of us would have uncharitably suggested that the smooth sward of Wembley would not have improved his ability either, but that may be too harsh. Anyway, Kevin slid around with the rest of them, including Middlesbrough's unlikely South American superstar, Juninho, who must have been asking himself which gods he'd offended to have allowed him to fetch up at a freezing St Andrew's for a Tuesday night League Cup replay. Kevin finds himself approaching the corner of their area with the ball bobbling around like an apple in a barrel of water and him looking as secure on his feet as … and I'll use it because, unoriginal as it is, it's what we always said about him … Bambi on ice. For one brief nanosecond, the stars aligned and somehow Kevin made a clean connection and rifled the ball into the net.

That victory, followed by another against Norwich, saw us into a two-legged semi-final against Leeds, who sat comfortably mid-table in the Premier League. The first leg was played at St Andrew's and although the pitch was marginally less uneven than the Middlesbrough game, it remained something of a challenge. As a brief side note, in terms of unparalleled advancement, the care and maintenance of pitches is now one of the wonders of the modern game and one that will play a part as the Blues approach the new century. Be that as it may, on another untrustworthy surface and against top-level opposition, we took the lead through another unlikely Kevin Francis screamer – executed on live terrestrial television for all the world to see. And that was as good as it got.

Leeds went on to overturn the lead and in the second leg brushed us aside, 3-0. As we left Elland Road, well beaten, Blues fans chanted to the effect that we hoped that Leeds would beat the Villa in the final and were roundly applauded by the home fans for so doing. All very amicable and fraternal. The silly bastards lost.

Kevin's League Cup heroics took place against a background of uninspiring mediocrity as the team meandered into 15th place in the league. By now, any magic dust that Fry may have brought with him had well and truly evaporated and his antics, once the source of tolerant amusement, seemed plain daft and a touch embarrassing. The owners knew this and so turned, as many of us hoped they would, to our one true legend of modern times, the real Francis – Trevor.

Trevor's managerial career, particularly prior to his appointment at Birmingham, will always be unfairly dogged by a relatively successful time at Sheffield Wednesday. First, he had his Dick Rowe moment. Dick Rowe? The guy from Decca who famously turned down the Beatles because he saw them going nowhere.

For Lennon and McCartney, read Eric Cantona. Trevor was given first dibs on Cantona but, having only seen him train on AstroTurf, wanted to see him on grass before committing to anything. Eric didn't take too kindly to this and threw in his lot with Wednesday's neighbours at Leeds where, it might be fair to say, he made something of an impact.

Trevor also pulled off something of a unique double. He guided Wednesday to both major cup finals – FA and League – in 1993, which is an undeniable achievement. Both were lost and both were lost to the same team – Arsenal. I think that can safely be called bittersweet. And it established Trevor as the nearly-man manager he became with Blues. He nearly got us promoted and he nearly won us the League Cup … but he didn't. He did forge the relationship with Steve Bruce, acquiring him as a player in a move which had lasting implications for the club, and he certainly knew a player when he saw one.

The team of the 90s which took us into the new century was littered with terrific talent. Up front there was the dynamic athleticism of Ndlovu, Furlong and Adebola. There was the ankle-biting menace of local boy Paul Devlin and the more refined ability of Brian Hughes. At the back, Bruce was joined by one of the iron-man brigade beloved by all supporters, Martin Grainger, whose toughness could only be marginally outshone by Martin O'Connor. The emerging talents of Andy Johnson and Darren Purse waited as Gary Ablett and dear old Kevin Francis moved on. We should have done better under Trevor. We had our moments, but they never came to fruition. But we were on the brink. Or the precipice. Or something.

Chapter 6

The century turns and we have something to cheer about

THE WORLD woke up on the morning of 1 January 2000 happy in the knowledge that the millennium bug had not destroyed the globe's communication systems and so we were still able to boil the kettle. The jury was still out as to whether things were really getting better in Blair's Britain, but the world certainly did not look as gloomily riven as it now appears to be. On the afternoon of the first day of this dawning millennium, Blues lost at home to Nottingham Forest to complete a dismal holiday period during which one point was gained from three games and we slipped from third to sixth in the table. The ramifications of this mini slump on the world's currency markets is not recorded.

Which is by way of saying that despite the determination of our teams to spoil weekends, holidays and family weddings, life goes on with these minor mishaps exposed as completely inconsequential. That's how we all try to kid ourselves, of course. Sometimes, we even do so. A good friend of mine, a Man City supporter, suffered the unendurable loss of a child.

In an article to which he contributed about football memoirs, he talks of how he knows that in the light of this it shouldn't have even crossed his mind how City were getting on at the time, let alone care about it, but he did. I'm sure there's a psychological study out there that explains this unhinged obsession on the part of so many of us and I'm sure it concludes that it's unhealthy behaviour. Like a true addict, I do know that it's nothing to be proud of but there's not a whole lot to be done about it.

Trevor's tenure as manager, as I explained in chapter 4, was marked by his degenerative relationship with the play-offs. Failure in 1999 against Watford was followed by catastrophe in 2000 against Barnsley when a 4-0 defeat in the home leg stunned even those of us accustomed to miserable failure. At the end of the 2000/2001 season came the Preston debacle which proved eventually to be the beginning of the end, even for the club's most favoured son. But before that happened, we flirted once again with the hint of glory and once again it was in the League Cup.

On 31 October 2000 I took a group of sixth-formers to the theatre in London. That was part of my job and one that I enjoyed. I had booked it well in advance and given that they were young adults, we were to travel on the tube. What I could not have known at the time of booking, however, was that after preliminary successes against Southend and Wycombe, we were to be drawn away at White Hart Lane to play Tottenham. The sort of evening away fixture that fans of clubs like ours crave. Professional commitments had to take precedence and so while I went off to watch *The Duchess of Malfi* (spoiler – she dies in the end) my wife was charged with taking my now committed Bluenose son to the game. For one final piece of context, this was in the pre-mobile era – just.

The play must have finished at about 10.30pm. It would not have been proper to have smuggled a radio into the theatre and so I remained entirely ignorant of events playing out seven miles further north. I had no positive expectations whatsoever but was looking forward to hearing family tales of treats and fun. As I walked between tube lines at Waterloo I spotted a guy in a Spurs scarf. Now to find out the miserable truth. 'How did your game finish, mate?' Steel yourself for complacent triumphalism. 'Lost. 3-1.' And off he grouched. I'd obviously misheard him. Or him me. This couldn't be true. So, I did what any sensible grown-up would have done in the circumstances. I waited for the next Spurs scarf and asked again. And it was true. I maintained proper calm in front of my charges in the face of this wonderfully unexpected news. In an example of execrable parenting, my son was allowed to stay up until I got home to share it all with me. What's more, it didn't turn out to be the highlight of the season: more success followed.

In the next round we beat Newcastle United, then of the Premier League, before eliminating Sheffield Wednesday, from our division, setting up a two-legged semi-final against the might of Ipswich Town. Yes, the might of Ipswich Town, who went on to finish fifth in the league. As a quick digression, the league was won easily that year by Manchester United, with their neighbours at City suffering one of their periodic relegations along with Coventry and Bradford City. For us, these were heady days indeed and a period when sides really did not want to come to St Andrew's on cold, foggy winter nights.

Football is the land of myths and clichés; it's part of our shared culture. The stats show, apparently, that both effete Fulham and loveable Swansea are harder places to prevail during winter evenings than Stoke, but that notion clings on all the same. My own memories of going to St Andrew's as a schoolboy on Tuesday nights are of relatively goal-filled victories against the poor saps trudging on to the pitch to be dismantled – one of the reasons that made the 1967 QPR League Cup debacle even more shocking. A great disappointment in researching for this book was that the facts didn't match these glowing memories, so my recollections must have been selective – which, when you support the likes of Birmingham City, must go down as some sort of self-preserving psychological phenomenon. All the same, the autumn and early winter of 2000 was a great time to be a home supporter.

Prior to the Ipswich semi-final games, Blues underwent the Christmas glitch referred to at the start of the chapter before embarking on a run of seven wins out of eight in the league, starting in January. Just in case we were in any danger of attaining one of the automatic promotion spots, we then contrived not to win for ten games after 14 March, condemning us once more to play-off purgatory. Prior to the start of the good run, we lost the first leg of the semi-final at Portman Road to a very dodgy penalty, but returning to St Andrew's on the back of a 1-0 defeat meant that the game was still very much alive. The second leg, on the last day of January, was a true epic.

It was a game played on a pitch the likes of which we never see at professional level any more. An attempt at defrosting it over the Christmas period, using something like pre-war industrial heaters, had left it scarred, rutted and uneven. It was entirely unsuitable for any sort of finessed ball-playing and, fortunately for us, this was Ipswich's strength, whereas strength was our strength. In the middle of the Horsfields, Adebolas, Graingers, O'Connors and Purses we had Danny Sonner passing the ball with occasional accuracy and

Stan Lazaridis flying down the wing, sometimes to good effect. It was Horsfield and Grainger who scored to turn the deficit around in front of a raging full house, only for Ipswich to score again and send the game into extra time.

To their great credit, both sides went to it with proper purpose in extra time, the possibility of penalties possibly proving a deterrent to the cautious tippy-tappy that so often suffocated such periods. As the game opened up on a surface that fast resembled a mole-infested meadow, Sonner found a proper pass through to Horsfield who finished with some style. This meant that there were now 17 minutes between us and an appearance in a major, proper final. It wasn't going to be at Wembley which was being refurbished, but at Cardiff's Millennium Stadium … but you kind of knew that somehow Ipswich were going to find the wherewithal to stop this from happening.

Then, with three minutes to go, an Ipswich player played an innocuous back pass to the keeper, Richard Wright. In a moment that would have been a living nightmare for him – and in a forerunner of the greatest goalkeeper howler of all time in front of the Tilton some two and a half years later – Wright air-kicked his clearance, aided by one of the many ruts gouged out in his penalty area. As the ball rolled under his foot – and I really, really don't want to have to employ this old chestnut – time did genuinely seem to stand still. There seemed to be a ball almost stationary in front of a completely unguarded goal. There seemed to be young Andy Johnson, on as a substitute, bearing down on it. And all he had to do was whack it into a completely empty net and we'd be going to the League Cup Final in Cardiff. There was no way that this could possibly be happening. Yet it was, and AJ duly booted the ball home for the easiest goal he'd ever score and in a moment that combined euphoria with disbelief, it dawned on us all that it was real. Hugging occurred.

Liverpool, who went on to finish third in the Premier League later that year, were to be our opponents in Cardiff. We set off on the day before the game, which took place on 25 February, for the monumental drinking session which was all part of a 'big day out'. Among my companions that evening was my son; he was 15 years old and he merits some pride of place in this book as he does, of course, in my heart forever.

As a woolly, liberal parent I always harboured the notion, in public at least, that should he grow up with no interest in football, I would live with that and encourage him with unbridled energy in whatever other pastime more closely mirrored his personality. In truth, of course, an early childhood littered with tiny footballs, magazines and other paraphernalia steered him inexorably in the direction of the beautiful game. The mini net in the back garden played a part.

In terms of affiliation, I was equally broad-minded and gracious, with the one stipulation being that as we lived within striking distance of the two top clubs in

North London and with Watford and Luton – Barnet even – offering viable alternatives, his choice should be more local and, what's more, I would take him there should he ever wish to go. I call that exemplary parenting – and I'm going to need to call on that as this part of the memoir develops, because, as you will have worked out by now, all of this openness and liberality on my part condemned him, born and bred 100 miles from St Andrew's, to the life of character building that is part and parcel of hitching yourself to mediocrity and non-achievement.

After a couple of years of hugely enjoyable ground-hopping as my own playing 'career' on a Saturday afternoon faded away, and after a brief flirtation with the glory to be had at White Hart Lane, he settled, to my enduring delight, on the Blues. For the record, he has turned out to be a personable, highly accomplished professional with his own wonderful family. My actions have not ruined him; he is the architect of his own frustrations.

On the evening of 24 February he was just a month past his 15th birthday and as we settled into the small hotel in Tintern where our travelling group was to spend the night, I explained in my most responsible sensible-parent tone that of course he could accept the occasional beer if offered, but to be careful and measured and that there was nothing creditable in drinking too much and making a fool of yourself. Stop, I told him, if you don't feel well.

You'll have worked it out; I'm not going to spell it out in all its unpleasantness. Suffice it to say that as I approach the end of my seventh decade, I am acutely aware of the fact that decay is setting in and it's only going one way. I try hard to deny these truths, but I reluctantly admit that I may require a degree of looking after in my approaching decrepitude. I had my first foretaste of that in a small Welsh village some 18 years ago, on glimpsing the mixture of wonderment and concern on my offspring's face when, after three attempts, I failed to get the key into the door of our bedroom.

When the fug cleared next morning, we enjoyed the carnivalesque atmosphere in Cardiff. Liverpool fans were graciously friendly and politely confident in their impending victory. We were still in night out mode, tempered for me by the fact that I would have to drive home that evening. The location of the Millennium Stadium, close to cafes, pubs and restaurants – so different from the concrete anonymity of Wembley, both old and refurbished – added to this air of occasion. Blues fans, as we did (spoiler alert again) when we went to the same final ten years later, got in early and savoured the stadium and our very presence at the event; who knew if and when we'd ever see its like again?

Liverpool's team was, naturally, littered with household names, always assuming you lived in a household that enjoyed football. The game was to be refereed by David Elleray, another big name. I'll get the naked prejudice out of the way from the start so that

Gil Merrick. Twenty-three caps for England and the first Blues manager on my watch. More widely remembered for shipping 13 goals against Hungary in two matches for England.

In the bath after Leyton Orient in 1972. Manager Freddie Goodwin makes a poor job of pretending to drink that champagne.

Alf Ramsey, looking as stiff and uncomfortable as ever. A young Trevor at his elbow.

Trevor Francis.

John Mitchell – before I knew his brother – wheels away after scoring in the FA Cup semi-final against us at Hillsborough in 1975.

Latchford, Francis and Hatton in the penguin shirt. Not sure it got any better. Note the letters for half-time scores.

Daft Kenny Burns. The player that all Birmingham fans would have been if they could.

Non-league Altrincham celebrate their FA Cup victory at St Andrew's.

Paul Tait and his famous shirt at the Auto Windscreens Final in 1995. A rare uncensored photo with the slogan fully visible.

Stern John wheels away in his sensible white vest having won the play-off semi-final at Millwall in 2002.

The boy Darren Carter scores the penalty that takes us to the Premier League in 2002.

Christophe Dugarry. He sparkled and shone – until he got bored and went home.

Enckelman reflects on his howler at St Andrew's ...but I still don't think he touched it.

Geoff Horsfield rounds the hapless Enckelman to score at Villa Park in March 2003.

A cup win. In my lifetime. A proper cup win.

Wild-eyed Lee Clark celebrates the great escape at Bolton in 2014.

0-8 at home. There's really nothing more to say.

Defeat at Tottenham in May 2011 sends us down. I've seen that look on our faces far too often.

readers can judge my assessment of his performance in the knowledge that for me he starts with a clear disadvantage. The video evidence of the crucial incident in the game is there for all to see; we'll come to it in a moment.

I should have a good deal in common with David Elleray. He is just a year younger than me and was a grammar school boy who went on to university (in his case, Oxford, so significantly more prestigious than my choice) and then went into teaching. Which should have made us the same sort of person ... except for the fact that Elleray chose to ply his pedagogic trade in the private sector – and at the top end of the private sector at Harrow. So, not proper teaching at all but a soft choice in a sector that continues to skew our educational system in favour of the already wealthy and privileged. OK. You can relax now. As I fully admit, that's the raw bias out of the way.

Thirty minutes into the game, Robbie Fowler scored an exceptionally good long-range goal to put Liverpool ahead. We'd been perfectly OK up to that point and there was nothing to suggest that the game was going to drift towards any sort of inevitable conclusion. And so it proved. Our platoon of hardmen plunged in and it took its toll in terms of injuries, but not without reward. Having kept the deficit to one goal, Blues mounted the sort of final charge of which we hoped they would be capable. In the final minute of the game, Liverpool defender Stephane Henchoz lunged into the clumsiest of challenges on Martin O'Connor and we had a last-minute penalty. Elleray had the bottle to award the penalty, albeit it couldn't have been a clearer decision, but failed to book Henchoz. O'Connor had to leave the field and all of our substitutes had already been deployed.

After a couple of penalty misses the season before, and much to our collective surprise, our regular penalty taker was now Darren Purse. Darren was a good old-fashioned, no-nonsense centre-half who chipped in with the occasional headed goal from set pieces and demonstrably gave of his best when playing for the Blues. His penalties had mirrored his style of play; hit as hard as possible and beyond the reach of the keeper. We weren't in the age of the Panenka and even if we had been, Darren wouldn't have taken any notice. Up he stepped after the lengthy delay while O'Connor's injury was dealt with and thumped his kick decisively into the net. Extra time. We had taken Liverpool to extra time.

And in extra time, we outplayed Liverpool. We did so with poor Martin O'Connor helplessly limping around in midfield trying to make a nuisance of himself, so playing, effectively, with ten men. With a minute to go before half-time in extra time, Elleray had his moment of shame. The unbooked Henchoz bundled Andrew Johnson over in another ungainly challenge in the penalty area. Elleray, the unashamed elitist that he was (OK, let me just have one more snipe) could clearly not allow himself to be the man who gave proletarian Birmingham City two penalties in a cup final, failed to award the spot kick, failed to book Henchoz – again – and primped off, waving away the protests of the enraged Blues players.

I'm writing this two months into the 2019/20 season in England. Football talk at the top level has become dominated by an increasingly tedious discourse around Video Assisted Refereeing – VAR. If you're now expecting me to come out with some guff along the lines of 'if only we'd had VAR', I'm afraid you are going to be seriously disappointed. Being a football supporter is built firmly on unfounded prejudice, unswerving and misplaced loyalty and, above all, a disposition – well, more like a willingness – to harbour and foment grudges for decades. We went on to lose that final on penalties. Oddly, in an echo of the golden goal final which had been the first to be decided in that way, this was the first major final to be decided on a shoot-out. I don't blame the two of our players who missed; these things happen. I blame Oxford-educated, public schoolmaster, pompous git, David Elleray.

Defeat at Cardiff did not seem to have an immediate effect on our form and we went on to win our next three matches before embarking on the disastrous run that saw us forgo any chance of automatic promotion and led us to the Preston calamity and the beginning of the end for Trevor.

When he left in the early autumn of the next season, it grieved me to hear some of the (entirely justifiable) criticism of his management prowess coming from the mouths and minds of those for whom he was not part of their history. His now dwindling media performances mark him out as a thoroughly decent and modest man and someone of whom we should all be proud.

His departure heralded the arrival of Steve Bruce, who even a mere 17 years ago, was half the very substantial man he now is. Brucey – yes, he was, for the most part, Brucey – had established an early reputation for being somewhat promiscuous in his managerial affections. We were his fifth club in three years. Since leaving us six years later he has managed a further six, including our unlovely neighbours. I've always liked him, notwithstanding his time across the expressway, but he is a man who has given the same post-match interview, especially after defeat, throughout his entire career: that little bit of luck what you need; I'm working very hard with these lads; these fans pay hard-earned money to come and watch this shite (that bit's not quite verbatim); all I can do is come to work every day and keep at it.

He came to us in the autumn of 2001 and about six months later, he did what Trevor had not been able to do: he got us into the play-offs and we were promoted. We finished up in Cardiff again but not before a night in Bermondsey that is now etched into the consciousness of all who were there.

And that, again, includes my offspring. We had drawn the first game against Millwall at St Andrew's and so the odds seemed to be against us. My son was smack in the middle of GCSE preparation and was suffering from a nasty cold and so we had to work hard together to persuade his mother that there would be no ill effects by getting some fresh air at a football match. I'd make sure he kept any shouting to a minimum and I'd whisk him home afterwards to be in bed in good time. It didn't quite work out like that.

In recent years the visit to Millwall has become almost genteel. There is a little gang of 16-year-olds who live on the upper terrace close to, but well protected from, the away end and this grouplet tries to relive the glory days of their reputation as hard-line hooligans. It's cringingly embarrassing but there's still just a hint of the general menace about the place that used to characterise this most unwelcoming of venues. The club has worked hard to shed the association with violence and racism that was definitely a part of its heritage and in recent years was at the forefront of working with community activists to save its local hospital. The walk through 'cowards' alley' – the walkway for away fans from South Bermondsey station to the ground – is not the fraught affair it once was. For all of that, on the evening of 2 May 2002, the place felt, well … naughty.

As far as the game was concerned, Dion Dublin – who will feature, bless him, in a future episode – missed a sitter for the home side. Stern John spurned a couple of clear chances for Blues and the game seemed to be drifting to extra time. The atmosphere throughout the game was edgy and both sets of supporters contributed to this through constant baiting. I'm not going to shake my head disapprovingly; it was plain brilliant. As was the stunning finale.

A right-wing corner in the last minute of the game was poorly dealt with by Millwall's defence. As the ball drifted out to the left it was cleanly crossed back in and knocked into the net by the same Stern John who had spurned those earlier chances. This all happened at the opposite end of the ground from us Blues fans and, in one of those oddities of perception, I will always recall that on scoring, Stern ripped off his shirt to reveal the sort of sensible white vest that your mother, and no one else, would urge you to don to fend off the ills and germs of inclement weather. At that point my paternal instincts somehow clicked in and I half-heartedly checked to see whether or not my croaking offspring was about to inflict irreparable damage on himself.

Blues saw the game through and then the fun well and truly started. To begin at the end, in the riot that followed – and it was a riot – Blues fans played no part. The head of the Metropolitan Police, Ian Blair, appeared on TV the next day and completely exonerated us. I'm sure there must have been a small constituency among our fans who registered a degree of disappointment about that. While cars burned, local residents cowered in their front rooms and daft lads chucked stuff at coppers, we were all safely locked in at The New Den, happily enjoying the distant chaos.

Apart, perhaps, from one anxious father who had vowed to return his examination-bound child to bed as soon as possible ... and whose wife may well have been anxiously following events on the telly. Eventually we were released to the background wail of sirens and marched on a bed of splintered glass between two rows of end-on-end police vans. We got home well past midnight but, as you will have picked up from an earlier reference, this stirring episode had no deleterious effect on my son's examination results. Phew.

And so back to the Millennium for the final against Norwich. If the Liverpool game had been a merry jaunt from which we had nothing to lose, this was a rather different affair. We were deemed to be slight favourites, but not even the most deluded among us would have thought this could make the slightest difference. Designated the most valuable game in world football because of the largesse to which the winners have access, the final was played in a rather peculiar atmosphere because the roof of the stadium was closed. The game was probably not a great spectacle for the neutral but when you're watching with nerves jangling and hoping against years of accumulated disappointment, it's impossible to make any such objective judgement.

No goals were scored after 90 minutes. In the first minute of extra time, Iwan Roberts put Norwich ahead but, miraculously, the wonderful Geoff Horsfield equalised 13 minutes afterwards and eventually the

match finished 1-1 and there would be a penalty shoot
-out. At Cardiff. Again. Well, that was that then.

They go first and score, but Stern John scores for
us. Then they miss and Paul Devlin scores for us. Then
they miss and Stan Lazaridis scores for us. Wait. Wait
a minute. We are in a penalty shoot-out in our biggest
game for decades. If we win it, we're going to go into
the Premier League. And we are winning it. When and
how is this going to go wrong? After three kicks each
we are two goals up. They take their fourth penalty and
score. That makes it 3-2 to us. This is where it unravels,
surely? But here's the deal. If we score the next penalty,
we win. We'll go up. Who's going to take it? Darren
Purse had not played in the final and our three best
strikers of a football had already taken theirs.

Step forward Darren Anthony Carter. Birmingham
boy, Birmingham City supporter, 18 years of age and
on as a substitute. Darren now does hilariously partisan
local radio coverage of Blues games and turns out for
Solihull Moors in the fifth tier of English football.
When he stepped up at Cardiff to take that crucial
penalty, he looked like what he was – a young, clean-cut
stripling straight from school. After a career around the
lower divisions, which never fulfilled our great hopes
in him, Darren now strolls imperiously in the Moors'
midfield looking like a Californian guitar hero from
the 70s who might just benefit from a more balanced
diet. To be honest, as far as all of us are concerned,
he could walk around the Bull Ring in a tutu over

camouflage gear and we'd still not even think about questioning his judgement. At around six o'clock on 12 May 2002, Darren Carter stepped up and planted his penalty beyond Rob Green and sent us into the top tier for the first time in 16 years.

A lithe Steve Bruce cavorted along the touchline. A season that had started with weary scepticism about Trevor's ability to take us forward had finished with a run of just two defeats in 15 games and success in the play-offs at last. It might be tempting to attribute this to some sort of Manchester United winning mentality that Bruce had brought with him, but his subsequent managerial career rather gives the lie to that idea. For the moment, such analysis was unnecessary.

The world was, indeed, a different place from the one at the start of the season. We had lost our first game of the season away to Wimbledon but won our next four to sit fourth in the table. Less than 72 hours after the fourth victory (2-0 at home to Sheffield Wednesday) crazy people flew planes into the twin towers in New York and we were all able to see football for what it was: a diversion and distraction from another set of events over which we felt little or no control, but the ramifications of which went a lot further than a worrying position in the league table.

But, hey, by May we were going up. Let the world burn for a while if need be. And for the first time in 16 years we were going to be playing the Villa in the top division. This might even turn out to be fun.

Chapter 7

We reach the promised land and create some memories

AS TONY Blair metaphorically licked George Bush's bottom and began to propel us into a disastrous war which has cast a shadow over the world since, Blues started to play in the Premier League. We were all prepared for the worst in both football and global geo-politics. A good mate at work snidely suggested that I enjoy my Premier League holiday and I wasn't confident enough to refute the idea that it might be anything more than that. We were both wrong. We lost our first two games, away at the Arsenal and at home to Blackburn, and at that point we were in the bottom three. It was the venerable Liverpool manager Bob Paisley who once advised us that it was foolish to look at the league tables until you needed an overcoat, so that early position didn't count. And after 24 August 2002 we never again entered the relegation places. It's true that for some time we bumped along very near the bottom, but we also had all the fun we had hoped for and more ... much, much more.

We were to have an early shot at the neighbours. Six games into the season and at home. For reasons only they could fathom, West Midlands Police allowed the game to be played on a Monday night just as the fat controllers at Sky had decreed. For most of us, particularly those who lived some distance from the ground, this meant the usual organisational arrangements for getting there after work. For others, not as constrained by inflexible wage slavery, it meant getting the day off and drinking yourself into a stupor. The evening of 16 September is engraved, very deeply, into the minds and memories of all who were there.

If you're unfeasibly impatient, you can use any old digital source to find out how the league table finished that season. Bear with me for a while though. The Villa had started the season with a couple of wins and three defeats. By the time we played them we had mustered our first win, against Leeds, and had drawn away at both Merseyside clubs; five games, five points, having played both Liverpool and Arsenal away. So far, so good. A point a game might just be enough to stay up – even though that didn't turn out to be the case in 2002/03. If you happen to use a well-known internet encyclopaedia you can also glance at another table – the newly established and universally ignored Fair Play League. We finished rock bottom and that is something about which those of us who even knew about it were very proud. Blues in 2002 were a tough old bunch and Bruce, who always acknowledged that Birmingham City was a working-class club with no frills, nurtured and encouraged this rough, musketeer spirit in his team. We bloody loved it.

And for a brief time in September 2002 we also loved our neighbours' manager, the genial and widely traduced Graham Taylor. Why? Simply because Taylor did not seem to have warned his players that they were about to enter something approaching a war zone, both on and off the pitch. For home supporters this was the chance, at last, for some revenge for all the condescension, arrogance and contempt we'd had to endure from Villa fans for years – all of which had been reheated and spewed at us through a number of cup defeats in the intervening period. Taylor didn't seem to have warned his players that this would manifest itself in incessant noise along with vitriolic, malicious jeering and massive personal abuse whenever the opportunity arose.

Perhaps the players themselves were insufficiently aware, or just plain complacent. That was certainly something that didn't last. Villa defender Olof Mellberg developed a deep-seated and very public hatred of BCFC and it must have stemmed from his involvement in the central event on that September evening in 2002. In the return game at Villa Park in March 2003 their players were visibly fired up, with hilariously self-destructive outcomes in which we will revel later in this chapter.

On the back of the noise and emotion at St Andrew's, Blues took the lead through Clinton Morrison. Clinton now plies his trade in the TV punditry business where his flamboyant dress sense and down-to-earth assessments have made him into a good turn. A south London boy with the accent to match, he was one of the many whose quirks of ancestry allowed him to turn out, with good effect, at international level with the Republic of Ireland. He always gave of his best for Blues and worked selflessly for his team-mates; and anyone who scores in a winning cause against the Villa was fine by us. Clinton's goal did shake the Villa out of their torpor and the game remained in the balance until the 77th minute when the crucial event occurred.

Mellberg took a throw-in on Villa's right and directed it towards his goalkeeper, Peter Enckelman, standing in front of an effervescent Tilton. In the time-honoured fashion, fans there let out the usual 'whhhhooooaaaa' in the forlorn hope that the keeper would miss the ball. And, of course, if Enckelman had missed the ball, it would have been inconsequential, the laws of the game dictating that a throw directly into the goal does not count. Now, brace yourself for what I still believe to be the truth. As the ball rolled tamely towards Enckelman and he put out his foot to trap it,

I think he missed it. I thought so at the time and I was sitting in the Main Stand just above the point at which Mellberg took the throw. I still think so now, every time I find myself laughing like a drain at the footage. But, the silly so-and-so only had himself to blame, because … as the ball rolled under his foot, Enckelman instinctively put his hands to his head as an admission of his horrible mistake. I still believe that this was the action that persuaded the referee that he had touched the ball and so the goal stood. It is entirely possible that in that moment of pandemonium, Enckelman forgot the laws of the game; I've heard plenty of stories about the way in which pros' understanding of them is tenuous at best. But the referee was convinced he'd touched it and gave a goal. And he was a good referee. One of the best in the land. So he must have been right. His name was David Elleray.

I honestly don't think for a moment that Elleray was righting the wrongs of the Millennium Stadium of 2001 and the Andrew Johnson penalty that he failed to award. I still harbour the grudge; that doesn't change. But for his part in allowing the goal on that night of nights, he is written indelibly into the history of Birmingham City Football Club. The over-privileged, pompous popinjay.

That was not the end of proceedings. Six minutes later, Geoff Horsfield scored again. So, before I slip unapologetically into cliché again, a word of explanation. For reasons that are too boring to go into, my season ticket was then in the Main Stand. When the Golds and Sullivan made good their promise to renovate St Andrew's, this resulted in three sides of the ground being modernised and, as a consequence, looking almost graceful. The Main Stand, squat, unlovely and built for another age, remained untouched. Parts of it fell off from time to time. Here were no concourses with state-of-the-art refreshment stalls. Stubborn, dingy kiosks lurked in stairwells. Toilets, difficult to locate, were small and eye-wateringly smelly. The clientele, as I have suggested elsewhere, veered to the senior end of the constituency. Chanting was unknown, singing a rarity and in my brief residence I found myself upbraided on many occasions for the use of profane language.

But when the Horse's goal went in that night, the old place shook. Genuinely shook. As the Railway End emptied of Villa fans, no one was in any doubt that we had been present on one of the great nights. The constabulary, too, might well have been grateful for the turn of events in the last quarter of an hour of the game. As the final whistle blew, the Railway was empty and, one imagines, the Villa fans were well on the road home. For that same police force, events six months later were significantly more challenging.

Once again, the match was earmarked by Sky for a Monday night. 3 March. 03-03-03. It was a clear omen, we told ourselves. We'd beaten them 3-0 and so it was destined to happen again. Of all the pre-match drivel and wishful thinking I'd heard over the years, this topped the lot. And what was clear from the kick-off was that the Villa weren't going to get fooled again. In many ways, their forced feistiness played into our hands. That kind of stuff was second nature to our lot, now enhanced by the unlikely addition of our World Cup winner, Christophe Dugarry. At this stage in his Blues career – he had joined in January – Dugarry was still very much in his falling over phase. So in between being kicked by Jeff Kenna, Robbie Savage, Damien Johnson and Stephen Clemence, the Villa's irritation was further enflamed by Dugarry acting like a dying swan as soon as anyone so much as shot him a nasty glance.

After a goalless first half, this all became too much for lovely footballer-turned-estate agent, Dion Dublin. He'd missed a sitter for Millwall in the play-offs and now he proved to be a gift that kept on giving. An altercation with Robbie Savage, right in front of the Blues supporters in the Witton End, finished with Dublin clearly pushing his head into Savage's. Referee Mark Halsey was not far away and had no hesitation in sending Dublin off. Cue the first of many scenes of mayhem at the Witton End over the next two years. Things got even better that night.

Just over 20 minutes later, Blues, who for some strange reason were playing towards the Holte in the second half, scored as Stan Lazaridis ducked to head in a bouncing cross from the right. Like I say, it was a long way away and so there was that moment familiar to all away fans in such situations when you can't be certain that it happened. Not least because the chance was taken by Stan finding himself in the middle of their goal – a position he never normally assumed – and also by the fact that he actually headed the ball. He was speedy, skilful and read the game well, but he was one of those blokes – and at parks level you find quite a few – whose neck seemed to telescope down into his torso when he tried to head a football. None of that mattered. We were a goal up against the Villa and they were down to ten men.

Three minutes later, a headed clearance from our defence sailed into the Villa half. The Horse went step for step with Jlloyd Samuel who sent a weakish header back towards his goalkeeper – yes, Peter Enckelman. The Horse, excuse the pun, wasn't even second favourite but Enckelman, this time without even the excuse of a roaring Tilton behind him, clearly lost his nerve. He opted to gather the ball with his hands but did so with the conviction of a vegetarian plunging his hands into the carcass of a chicken. This time he definitely did touch the ball and succeeded in pushing it into Horsfield's path, who strolled towards a disbelieving Holte End to deposit the ball into an empty net.

Two up, 13 minutes to go, Villa down to ten. But this didn't last. Four minutes later, Villa's Joey Gudjonsson lunged into a tackle on Matthew Upson and received his second yellow card – although the challenge probably merited a red on its own. Many of the following morning's papers, including the broadsheets, chose to use terms such as 'chaos' and 'mayhem'. Frankly, that was underplaying it. The dismissals of Dublin and Gudjonsson were rendered doubly delicious by the fact that the players' tunnel, down which they were obliged to disappear, is on the corner by the away fans. Yet even as the second of these was waved a cheery goodbye, the drama was far from over.

With just a few moments to go, Blues keeper Nico Vaesen was injured. Unlike at St Andrew's, the ground had not emptied and the atmosphere, particularly as numbers of Villa fans somehow managed to gravitate towards the away supporters, was becoming more malignant by the minute. It became clear that Vaesen could not continue and Blues had used all their substitutes. As riot police began to surround the crowd, Geoff Horsfield donned the green jersey and the gloves to see the game out. It was, by now, plain barmy.

With all of the shenanigans over this prolonged injury, the turmoil around the two sending offs, as well as the two goals, there had to be at least six or seven minutes of time added on. Someone else who was present may be in a position to contradict me on the first part of what follows, but definitely not the second. In all the confusion, I'm pretty sure that no board went up with the number of minutes on. Like I say, I'm prepared to be contradicted on that. What is beyond debate is that after 92 minutes, referee Halsey blew the final whistle with no ceremony or flourish and got the players off the park as quickly as possible.

To our great delight we were forced by West Midlands's finest to remain in the ground. Outside, reminiscent of The New Den ten months earlier, sirens wailed. Once released from the ground and in possession of a 16-year-old (now with a hatful of GCSEs), I made for our car as unobtrusively as possible. The record shows that there were plenty of arrests but, once again, our job was to get home safely. Given my own almost uncontainable excitement, I knew that a 100-mile drive was going to be a challenge, so I deliberately worked on dampening down my emotions. I swear to this day that I don't remember driving home. Five weeks later I was 50. I'll leave that there.

Other things happened in our first season in the Premier League and they were genuinely exciting. In the fixture prior to the Villa game in March we had beaten Liverpool at home, which was just as well because in the eight games prior to that we had managed only three draws along with five defeats. The holiday period had not been kind to us, pitting us against Manchester United (eventually champions that year), Leeds and Arsenal – all of whom disposed of us with some ease. The last of these games merits special mention because I had never allowed myself to react to a home defeat as I did on 12 January 2003.

Up until that point in the season, with the exception of the point gained at Anfield, we had not troubled any of the big boys. Bruce had made it clear – and it was a point fully understood by all of us – that if we were to survive in the top division, it was from the teams round the middle and bottom that we needed to garner points. Anything else was a bonus. Prior to the Arsenal game, we had 25 points and were in 15th place; far from secure, but perhaps more comfortable than we expected to be. And we'd beaten the Villa. It is a measure of the unfounded optimism that sustains the idiotic football fan that we always hope that today will be the day. Today will be the day that the Arsenal will come to St Andrew's and we're on the telly and we'll turn them over.

We were 2-0 down before the half hour. That's happened before and it will happen again. Usually at that point, you say to yourself that all is not lost, one more and we're in it. It had already happened at Anfield – Steven Gerrard, Michael Owen and all. But sitting there watching the Arsenal playing football from another planet, even the most deluded of romantics knew that all hope was lost. Our first reaction was to hope that they'd go easy on us and not humiliate us too cringingly on national TV. When it became clear that they weren't busting a gasket to do so, for the first and only time in my life when watching the Blues, from about an hour in, I relaxed and enjoyed watching the opposition. They won 4-0 and went on to finish second in the table behind United. Next season they went through the season unbeaten. If you'd been at

St Andrew's that afternoon, you wouldn't have been surprised.

Bruce's strategy of targeting those around us paid dividends. A sensational home win against Liverpool prior to the Villa game in March had unexpectedly stopped the winter rot and following the riotous night at Villa Park, another four wins out of six, mainly against the teams around us, assured us of a glorious end to the season. This would probably not have happened had it not been for the fact that for half a dozen games in March and April 2003, dashing, exotic World Cup-winner Christophe Jerome Dugarry decided to play out of his skin for Birmingham City and pretty well won a few games on his own.

On Easter Monday at Charlton he scored with a cheeky back-flick. Really? A Birmingham City player scoring with a back-flick? In the following game at St Andrew's – one that I was forced to miss and have regretted doing so ever since – a sensational free kick, in what was universally recognised as one of the most exciting matches there in years, is there for all to see, along with the flick, on YouTube. By the time he scored again in the next game against Middlesbrough – a nonchalant Gallic volley, having controlled the ball on his silky thigh – he had scored five goals in four games and we were well and truly safe. Yet there were still two further glorious parts to the conclusion of this season.

The Albion had suffered one of their periodic nightmare seasons and were relegated with a measly

26 points – not as measly as bottom-placed Sunderland who, during one of their own occasional slumps, had acquired a mere 19. The last relegation place was still up for grabs and it was between West Ham and Bolton. And on the final day of the 2003 season, the former, with all their own World Cup associations of glory, to which the soft-brained among them clung with the pathetic nostalgia of Nigel Farage and his ancient, grey Brexiteers, came to St Andrew's needing to better the result of their northern rivals. To be absolutely clear: another side was coming to us on the last day of the season to avoid relegation and we were completely safe. What, as they say in modern parlance, was not to like?

For a few brief moments, with 25 minutes to go, Bolton just 2-1 up and West Ham having taken the lead, their massed fans in the Railway had some hope. I'd like to think that our own players, understanding that accusations of last-day laziness would be coming their way, stirred themselves into action and late goals from the Horse and Stern John put us in the lead. Crazy-man Paulo di Canio equalised for West Ham with two minutes to go, but with them now needing a winner and Bolton needing to concede twice to Middlesbrough, the game was up and we sent them down. We were gracious in our mutual applause as groups of fans but on this rare occasion we could afford such magnanimity.

West Ham had been unlucky. The received wisdom has always been that 40 points pretty well assures you of safety. This is not borne out statistically. Sunderland went down in 1997 with 40 points, as did Bolton a year later. When West Ham went down that day in 2003, they had 42 points. Yet, no other team has had to come remotely close to that total to stay up since. The only team that has needed 40 points, the team with the highest points total required since that day in 2003, the team that went down with 39 points when 34 and 35 had been enough in previous seasons was, in 2011 … oh, finish it off for yourselves.

But on 11 May 2003 we finished in 13th place with 48 points, three points and three places above the Villa having beaten them twice. Our owners seemed to be backing us, we appeared to be solvent and we might even be building something for the future. The next few years, as the great powers embarked on proxy wars across the globe and failed to see all the warning signs of the impending banking crisis for which we're all still paying, could yet turn out to be good ones for BCFC. And for a brief, surprising period, they were.

Chapter 8

We think we might belong in the top flight, but we're not quite sure

AT THE start of the 2003/04 season, Blues bought well and acquired a gem of a loan. The purchase was David Dunn from Blackburn and the loan was Mikael Forssell from Chelsea. The former always looked a tad stout but possessed great touch and passed the ball as well as many of us could remember from a Blues player.

Regrettably, he appeared to have muscles and ligaments made of cheese and so his reputation as an injury risk turned out to be fully deserved. All the same, he could light up a game and in a season in which we won four and drew two of our six opening fixtures, he demonstrated this great talent which, from time to time, he replicated in the future.

Forssell scored goals. He scored 19 of them that season and always looked a threat. It was a measure of the talent available in Chelsea's ever-growing empire that they felt they could dispense with such ability. The acquisition of Forssell became even more significant as Dugarry's star faded rapidly. Possibly exhausted by his heroics at the end of the previous season but, more likely, just a touch bored, he never really shone again. He managed only one more goal in a losing cause against Charlton at home – no cheeky back-flick on this occasion – and was released from his contract in March. He had illuminated the club for a brief while and his talent was extraordinary. All the same, those who identify him as the greatest Blues player of the modern era need to acquire a sense of perspective.

Throughout the autumn of 2003, Blues hovered between fourth and fifth place in the Premier League. I almost feel I should have written that in capital letters, as unprecedented as it was. As it turned out, it represented a high spot not yet replicated. When the Villa came to St Andrew's in October they were ten places below us and when the final whistle blew on a dull 0-0 draw, their fans celebrated as if it had been a victory. To all of us, that reaction seemed to indicate that there was a possibility that the order of things could really be changing.

We were wrong. By the time of the return fixture in February, Villa were under the more competent management of David O'Leary and a couple of places above us in the table, albeit with only one more point. By then, we had slipped to tenth. Sorry ... but I have to repeat it: *slipped* to tenth. If we were harbouring concerns that the bubble might soon be about to burst, that felt ever more likely when they went 2-0 up just before the hour. But we did score a goal and were back in the game. All Blues fans know what happens next, but just for the neutral (and make sure you watch it online too) ... with seconds left in added time and the whistles from the Villa fans rising to ear-splitting volume, Darren Purse hoofs the most hopeful of punts into the Villa area. Forssell wins the header, there is a scramble in the goalmouth, the ball falls to Morrison whose shot is parried by Villa keeper Sorensen and there, lurking, as he was at Millwall a couple of years earlier, is Stern John. I'm still pretty sure he nearly mishits it. He'd only been on the field for ten minutes but in it goes in front of the Blues fans in the Witton who go bonkers. For the record, Stern must have been having style lessons, because as the shirt comes off on this occasion, gone is his mum's recommendation of sensible underwear, to be replaced by a smart blue tee shirt. Possibly not the most important detail from this most dramatic of denouements, but worth a mention.

The Villa game came in the middle of a run of eight games undefeated and the possibility of a finish that would provide European football was now on the cards. However, after winning at home against Bolton on 6 March, Blues only managed one more victory all season, gaining eight points from the remaining 11 games and finishing in tenth place. Very Birmingham City. The Villa finished sixth.

In the final game of the season, Blues travelled to Blackburn for a game on which nothing was riding … oh, how we sometimes long for such occasions – but not too frequently, mind. In goal for Blackburn was one Peter Enckelman. Someone at Rovers must have had a wicked sense of humour because he only ever played three games for them in four years. Whether it was his choice to come out and lay the ghost of Birmingham City or a locker-room jape, only his memoirs will reveal. We sang his name throughout and when, in the second half, he came to take his place in front of us, he cheerily acknowledged the joyful reception which he was afforded. Stern John's late equaliser (yep, one of those again) was not his fault and at the final whistle he turned as he left the field to applaud and smile at his tormentors. The season had ended with relative disappointment, but that was a properly memorable moment.

We had survived two seasons in the top flight under Bruce's leadership. He gave the clear impression that he liked the club and the supporters and his media appearances were never too much of an embarrassment. He was now entering dangerous territory for all managers in whatever league they operate: taking the club to the next level. The lower divisions of English football are littered with the detritus of those who have overreached in this way and, as time has revealed only too clearly, Bruce as a manager experiences a kind of nosebleed when he gets anywhere near the top half of the Premier League. His brave attempt at making us more Barcelona than Brum never got off the ground in a season characterised by some notable comings and goings.

The first one to come was Emile Heskey. Goodness only knows how his self-esteem endured the early terrace ditty that suggested that there was only one Emile Heskey, who used to be shite, but now was alright, but it did and, notwithstanding the unwarranted opprobrium that seemed to dog his entire career, he scored important goals and worked hard. Bruce also took on a slew of players who were either past their sell-by date or nudging that particular safety line: Dwight Yorke (never a favourite with his Villa associations), Darren Anderton and Mario Melchiot. To join his old chum, Robbie Savage (more follows), Muzzy Izzet was acquired. He played ten games, in one of which he was sent off, before injury ensured that he never played for us again. And we brought in tricky Danish international winger Jesper Gronkjaer from Chelsea.

Gronkjaer was lightweight and looked an increasingly forlorn figure in the dozen or so games he lasted. What was worse, sections of the crowd started getting at him. Such instances are far from unknown among football supporters. As I take my seat each season, I ponder who will turn out to be the target of the wags and miseries who sit around me. Who will be this season's waste of time, space and money and I pay my wages to watch you, you clown, just get it forward, call yourself a professional footballer, you complete fucking tosser. I'm sure you get the picture. As I will soon reveal, I am not innocent in this regard.

What marked out the treatment of Gronkjaer as different was that for the first time since promotion, the cheerful solidarity from the terraces began to fracture, probably as a result of raised expectations and possibly because of a newer, less battle-hardened sort of supporter. It augured ill for any attempt at becoming expansive and attractive. Nonetheless, the 2004/05 season, in which we finished 12th, was one of the very few since the turn of the century where anything approaching stability at the club looked possible.

Over at Blackburn Rovers, Peter Enckelman was bench-warming and unlikely to dislodge US international, Brad Friedel. He must have watched both Blues–Villa games with an ever-expanding smile of relief. Goalkeeper Thomas Sorensen tried his very best to supersede him in our affections. In December at Villa Park he allowed a tame, bobbling shot from Clinton Morrison to bounce over him and into the net. Villa 1, Blues 2. The following March, his creaky dive and slippery handling allowed a marginally better effort from Emile Heskey to creep over the line. Blues 2, Villa 0.

Sorensen will never attain Enckelman's hero status – it's still not rare to see Blues fans with his name on the back of their replica shirts – but he gave it a proper go. All the same, when the players left the field at St Andrew's on 20 March 2005 on the back of a Blues victory, I think those in claret and blue, whether playing or watching, would have settled for the fact that they had endured the last league defeat at the hands of Small Heath until at least 2020 … facts are correct at the time of going to press.

Other than these local triumphs, the season was notable for two league victories against Liverpool and a run of four consecutive wins over the Christmas holiday period which settled us in mid-table – where we remained in unspectacular comfort. The second of these victories was at home against Middlesbrough on Boxing Day. Heskey and Morrison scored in a 2-0 victory, but the game will be remembered more for one wonderful comic moment.

Up front for Boro was one Mark Viduka. Although 30 and approaching the end of a highly creditable career, Viduka – who could never have been described as lithe – had, to be brutally candid, let himself go a bit. He was still a handful and had a good goalscoring record, but he was clearly a man who was no stranger to a buffet. After about 20 minutes he hit the deck with what looked like a strain or a pull. A merrily lubricated St Andrew's yule crowd all enjoyed the moment, not least because he was a good player and it looked like he was having to go off. Our jollity was increased when it became apparent that he was going to need a stretcher and that some poor saps were going to have to lift him on to it and carry him from the pitch. As they attempted the first part of this exercise a huge groan of 'Heeeaaavee' filled the ground as poor old Mark Viduka endured being carried from the field of play. Instead of enjoying the usual sympathetic round of applause, he was serenaded by laughter and observations about the task he was inflicting on the buckling first-aiders.

Over at the Hawthorns on that same Boxing Day – 42 years after my Uncle Lou had tried to save me – the Albion were being thumped 5-0 by Liverpool. Thus, they were bottom at Christmas with ten points from 19 games. History dictated that they must go down. But on the final day of the season, they went into their home game with Portsmouth needing to win and for the most convoluted set of results to occur for them to survive. So, while were enjoying ourselves beating a cup final-bound Arsenal, attention was focussed down the Soho Road.

I part company with some Blues fans here. There is a widely held view, possibly a majority position, that says that the Albion are not the Villa and, therefore, not the enemy. The argument goes that their fans, like ours, although largely from a different part of the city and beyond, are working class, loyal and without pretensions. Yes, they may have enjoyed relatively more success than us, but that is largely in the past and, like us, they've been up and down more often than a bride's nightie. (Please – it's just a silly joke.) I've never been convinced. During the 70s they had exciting players and a decent set-up. There's no doubt that the club played a huge part in the fight against racism in their support for Regis, Batson and Cunningham. Maybe it's just the inherently grudging nature of all dyed-in-the-wool Blues fans, but I've always found them just a touch arrogant; not Villa arrogant, but enough to dispel any warm sentiment towards them.

As Emile scored a last-minute winner against the Arsenal, news continued to come from across the city and the airwaves that the Albion had, in fact, defied history and stayed up. Those so inclined were further cheered by the fact that Geoff Horsfield had scored one of the goals that had set them on their way. It was a decent enough way to end 2005 before we embarked on six years of utter turbulence.

The tone for that turbulence may well have been set in train by the antics of Robbie Savage. To be clear from the start, Savage played his heart out for Blues and had been instrumental in our relative success and development. Anyone who attempts to argue otherwise either wasn't paying attention or didn't go to games. His mark as a player, both with us and everywhere else he has played, was that he was honest, hard-working and made the most of what ability he had. That he has taken these qualities into an unlikely media career speaks highly of his determination and a degree of self-awareness that seems to swing between being non-existent and ironically savvy.

In the winter of 2004/05 he lost the plot, as did the club in its dealings with him. He manufactured a cock and bull story about living nearer to his parents instead of just saying that he wanted to join his friend, Mark Hughes, at Blackburn. Bruce and the club's management handled the situation with all the aplomb of a nervous new teacher confronted by his/her first very naughty boy (believe me, I know of what I speak) and in the end, a good servant of the club departed under an unnecessary cloud.

As the Savage saga unfolded, we brought in Jermaine Pennant, electronically tagged on the back of a drink-driving conviction, and the Uruguayan, Walter Pandiani. If you google the latter, the word 'truck' almost inevitably crops up in the search box. He liked a big truck and he drove one both to training and to home games at St Andrew's. It was huge. There was something oddly eccentric in all of this that appealed to the looniness of Blues supporters. Like Pennant, his career with us was short, but speckled with occasional highlights. In his 32 appearances he scored six goals – all against the very top clubs, with the exception of one on his debut against Southampton. Pennant did enough in his time with us to earn a move to Liverpool, where he flourished for a while before sliding down the leagues and into comfortable obscurity.

Savage's departure, though, marked the end of the era of Blues as the plucky, scruffy, dislikeable underdog, there to spoil the party. We were off on a bumpy old ride.

Chapter 9

In which we are, indeed, the bride's nightie

FIRST, THE bare, mind-boggling facts. On 26 April 2006 with a minute to go in the penultimate game of the season, Mikael Forssell missed a good chance to win the game against Newcastle at St Andrew's. The match finished goalless and so with one game to go at the end of a miserable season of drudgery and non-achievement, our four-year stay in the Premier League came to an end. Five years later, on the final day of the season at Tottenham, we went down again. In the intervening period we had been promoted twice and relegated once more.

Put another way, we only had two consecutive seasons in the same division. Strangely, only two managers oversaw this dizzying time: Steve Bruce and Alex McLeish. Crucially, the ownership of the club changed just once.

Given the volume of newsprint, social media chatter and wall-to-wall TV coverage of football, most of which purports to afford us insights into how clubs are run and who's moving and shaking, the plain fact is that most people, 'insiders' included, know nothing of how a football club conducts its daily affairs. There is always a trail leading to the culprits when things eventually go wrong and the financial house of cards on which the whole game teeters and tumbles down. But for the rest of the time, convenient and lurid dramas are woven and presented to those of us who are prepared to suspend our disbelief.

All of which is a prelude to saying that by the middle of the decade, the Golds and Sullivans, guided by Brady's alleged business acumen, appeared to be losing interest in the good people of Birmingham (if they ever had any) and patience with honest, reliable, but limited, Steve Bruce. Lurking in the shadows was Hong Kong 'businessman' and hairdresser, Carson Yeung – a man, apparently, laden with gold and driven by an ambition to make Bordesley the centre of the football universe. The Gullivans didn't feel like asking too many questions when Yeung offered them some £80 million for the club, presumably because they were too busy snickering up their sleeve. It was a ridiculous over-valuation, but why should they have cared?

Off they went to their apparent first love, West Ham United, where some four years after they left

Birmingham, they pulled off an astonishing financial coup by acquiring the public asset of the Olympic Stadium for their private use and the acquisition of yet more money for themselves. Carson Yeung – well, would ya believe it – turned out not to have any proper money at all and ended up in jail, which, given the propensity of wronged financiers from that part of the world to find innovative ways of exacting funds from debtors, may have been the safest place for him.

Meanwhile, in the nether regions of the known physical world, in a dim, cobwebby dungeon, something called the Fit and Proper Persons Committee – there to protect clubs and supporters through their brave and decisive actions – met to count mythical beans and scratch plans with their overgrown fingernails on the damp walls.

Long before any chance of survival disappeared with Mikael's uncharacteristic miss, the season had been stamped as one of utter disaster. Somehow Bruce survived it and to his great credit managed to convince the owners to keep him on – faith which he repaid by guiding Blues to immediate promotion the year afterwards.

By the time the clocks went back in 2005, we were 19th, saved from bottom place by the complete shambles at Sunderland, who only managed to squeeze out 15 points all season. It was also one of those years when it was the Albion's turn to go down. From late October onwards, Blues were only out of the bottom three for one week. In between times, shocking stuff happened.

First, as if in some kind of telling omen, we lost to the Villa for the first time since promotion in 2002. It was at home in October by one single goal. The scorer merits his own section. He may well have forgotten me by now, but I have followed his career with great interest and admiration.

Kevin Mark Phillips is rightly admired as one of the best goalscorers in English football. His England career was all too brief, particularly in an era when the national team wasn't actually sparkling in the firmament; he played eight times for his country and, surprisingly, given his overall record, failed to score. However, in 580 other appearances, he scored 246 times and was, especially in the penalty box, accurate and lethal. Between 2005 and 2011 he hawked himself around all three Birmingham clubs – Villa, Albion and Blues – scoring 61 times in 163 appearances. And I taught him.

Let's be clear. I taught him English and while he was always a pleasant and well-disposed young man, I doubt he ever saw the acquisition of GCSE English as anything more than one of life's necessary irritants. I can claim not one iota of credit for nurturing his footballing prowess. What's more, when he turned out for the annual school vs teachers game in his senior year, none of us knowing parks lumberers had him down as anything special, despite the fact that we knew that clubs were sniffing around him. I'll leave that there as comment on my ability to spot a player when I see one.

Unknown to him, he had a moment of revenge – albeit not quite as devastating as his goal in front of the Tilton for the Villa in October 2005. At the height of his career he had been interviewed by a football publication in the vein of a questionnaire that elicited answers such as *'Godfather II'* and 'steak and chips'. When asked if he had a favourite book, Kevin replied to the effect that he wasn't much of a one for reading. A friend spotted this and gleefully sent the cutting to me as proof of my hopeless prowess as a teacher. So, as I say, I had a strong but entirely non-influential connection to the man who broke Blues' three-year spell over the Villa. Incidentally, Thomas Sorensen played in goal for the Villa that day and, in further proof that times had changed, put in a safe and convincing performance.

Just for human interest and to tell one of the saddest football stories I know, I'll loiter to tell the tale of another of my pupils who made it as a professional footballer. Ross Flitney was a well-mannered individual who quietly and sensibly combined study with his sporting ambition. He was a goalkeeper and was courted by top sides during his time at school. As is often the case, this played out with Ross eventually earning his living in the lower reaches of the professional game; in 2005 he signed for Barnet, then in the fourth tier of English football. In October 2005, Barnet had the good fortune to draw Manchester United at Old Trafford in one of the early rounds of the League Cup.

Eighty seconds into the game, United played a rather hopeful ball forward and Ross came to the edge of his area to collect it. In a moment of eagerness, unthreatened by any oncoming forward, he reached beyond the extent of his area to gather the ball in. A silly, nervous mistake on the biggest night of a 21-year-old's career. No real damage, no goalscoring opportunity denied. A quick word from the ref: 'Big occasion, son. Watch your step.' Afraid not. Hidebound, no doubt, by this week's pronouncement from the men in blazers, referee Richard Beeby decided that this merited a red card. The quickest ever issued at Old Trafford. For an action born of nothing more than harmless nervousness. I'm not sure if Ross has ever had need of his GCSE English, but wherever he is, I wish him well.

I certainly didn't wish Kevin Phillips well when his characteristically pinpoint shot went in, although some time further on, his precious goals for Birmingham City were applauded to the rafters. Villa went on to complete the double over us that year, winning 3-1 at Villa Park in April. Our goal that day was scored by current self-styled media provocateur, Chris Sutton, who only managed a few games for us before following Robbie Savage into unwarranted prominence on the airwaves. By then, however, the game was as good as up, albeit Villa's victory that day pretty well assured their own survival in a dull season for them. Immediately above Blues in the safety of 17th were Portsmouth who we had drubbed 5-0 at the start of the year, before loveable villain 'Arry Redknapp brought his very own financial stardust to that club, setting them on the road to perdition. We'd get to know him at close quarters soon enough.

Portsmouth survived with 38 points, but we could have no complaints. We had scraped out a wretched 34 with only eight wins all season. We scored 28 goals in 38 games. And as if that wasn't bad enough, we really did make complete arses of ourselves on national TV.

Despite this most grim of seasons, we somehow stumbled along in the FA Cup to reach the sixth round – the final eight. Who knew? Maybe we could salvage something from this wreckage. Bruce himself made all the right noises about this with some arcane comments about smelling hot dogs at Wembley, and although our opponents were to be high-flying Liverpool, we were at home and it was, as cliché has it, the FA Cup where anything could happen.

What did happen was that within five minutes we were two down. So that was that. A third Liverpool goal before half-time absolutely sealed the deal. At that point – especially as we were being paraded for the nation's delectation – it had to be damage limitation. Didn't it? Sides eased off when the game was wrapped up like this, particularly big sides like Liverpool with their rotations and restings and recovery periods and an eye on bigger prizes. Didn't they?

7-0. On TV. On a work evening.

It wasn't as if I hadn't been close to such utter disappointment before – the number of goals may have differed, but the spectre of the QPR disaster nearly 40 years earlier still hovered. We may not have expected to beat Liverpool, but this was, after all, a side in our own division. They went on to win the cup and finish third in the league, one place below Manchester United, which is where we went to play on the Sunday following the drubbing – and, once again, on TV. I was just about brave enough to watch sitting on, as opposed to behind, the sofa as we kept it to an eminently respectable 3-0 defeat. That's what life as a Blues supporter looked like in the spring of 2006, just before the Villa joyfully despatched us and as Bruce made error of judgement upon error of judgement until we were finally put out of our misery.

Brucey found himself back home in the second tier, probably where his managerial heart and soul resided. Quite how and why he was still in a job remained a mystery, but he stayed in post and did what he was supposed to do. At the start of the 2006 season he acquired the services of three Arsenal loanees: Sebastian Larsson, who turned out to be an absolute diamond for Blues and Sweden, Fabrice Muamba, later to acquire fame for all the wrong reasons when his heart gave out on the field of play, and Nicklas Bendtner, who was extremely talented but whose arrogance was only outweighed by his lack of self-awareness. Think I'm overstating it? Read the next anecdote and then watch the highlights of the game to which it refers.

After an indifferent start to the season, Blues were seldom out of the top places. In April we went to play Wolves at Molineux needing a win to go top. Wolves themselves had slipped a little but were still in with a chance of automatic promotion. The term 'classic' when applied to football matches is overused; not on this occasion.

After a first half in which Wolves dictated the play, Blues were indebted to goalkeeper Colin Doyle for keeping them in the game. The second half was mayhem. Blues took the lead (ex-England international Andrew Cole, acquired by Bruce in the final games to give that little bit of extra what you need) only for Wolves to score twice – a lead they held until the 78th minute. Bendtner then scored with a thunderous header from a corner before quarter of an hour of madness ensued. First, Cameron Jerome scored what looked like a winner with two minutes to go; we will return to the details of this shortly. On 91 minutes Wolves were awarded the sort of mystery penalty that sometimes occurs when even players don't appeal for anything. First place and automatic promotion within touching distance were going to be snatched away … until, in a genuine hugging-strangers moment, Doyle saves the penalty, Blues see out the remaining two minutes and an absolutely epic fixture finishes – except for those of us who have to negotiate the unlovely streets of Wolverhampton and potential ambush from disgruntled Dingles.

So, to Jerome's goal and Bendtner's kind of part in it. Cameron Jerome was a trier of the first order and a player with more talent and ability than is generally recognised, particularly by the bonehead who sits three rows behind me for whose great wit and wisdom he was a regular target. He scored 113 goals in his 470 league appearances for various clubs but, to be unsympathetically accurate, he possibly missed at least three times as many, especially in one-on-one situations. Which is where, with two minutes to go against Wolves and the sides level in a crucial top-of-the-table game, he found himself on 22 April 2007.

Not to worry. He had broken free of the Wolves back four and as he homed in on goal, all he had to do was square it to one of the two Blues players in the area and it was job done. But he didn't. Approaching from the corner of the penalty area, he slid the ball under the keeper and to everyone's joy and astonishment, finished the job himself. Everyone, that is, apart from Nicklas Bendtner who, even as the ball goes in the net, stamps his foot and turns to Jerome in fury for not passing it to him to score.

For a while, Bendtner attracted a cult following in his native Denmark dubbing him 'Lord' and 'Emperor'. In 2018 he was sentenced to 50 days in jail for assaulting a taxi driver. It is universally accepted in footballing circles that he never truly fulfilled his potential. Cameron Jerome, on the other hand, has gone about his business in a way that has earned him little other than admiration for his dedication and hard work. As I've mentioned before, it's best not to think about the personal qualities of a bloke with whom you are briefly in love in the instant that he scores a goal for your team, but who is, all too often, a complete bellend. But I'd like to think that honest Cameron might be better than that.

The end of that season was also notable for a huge favour done for us by another old flame – Clinton Morrison. With a couple of games to go, the two automatic places were undecided: Blues had 83 points, Sunderland 82 and Derby 81. On the penultimate weekend of the season, Sunderland played on the Friday and won – 85 points. Blues played on the Saturday and, with ten men and a stunner from Seb Larsson, beat Sheffield Wednesday – 86 points and top of the table with one game to go but, astonishingly, not assured of promotion. Derby were to play Palace on the Sunday. Win and they were still in it and we had work to do; any other result and we were up.

There is an enduring myth among football supporters about sides being 'on the beach'. We'll be OK, we convince ourselves, because we only need a point to stay up/get into the play-offs/ensure promotion because our opponents have 'nothing to play for' and are just there to make up the numbers. To their great discredit, some lazy journalists often cite such windy rubbish. I can only assume that such people never even turn out with their mates for even the friendliest of five-a-sides at their local leisure centre. Nobody who plays sport in an organised way, especially for a living (I assume), likes losing. I have no idea what the stats reveal for games when teams who are supposedly lining up their pina coladas are pitted against those for whom the stakes are higher, but I doubt that there's any pattern of weak capitulation on their part. All the same, to my shame, I was convinced that Palace would be on the beach and that we were in for a very nervy final weekend.

So, when Clinton scored with a neat finish on 29 minutes to put Palace ahead, although I didn't celebrate with quite the fervour as I had done when he did the same against the Villa five years earlier, it was still a great moment. Interviewed afterwards, Bruce – who had decided that Clinton was surplus to requirements at Birmingham and so had sanctioned his sale to Palace – claimed that he had sent him a text of gratitude to which Clinton had graciously replied. Whether or not any of that was true, Palace's eventual 2-0 win made it an uncharacteristically relaxed end to the season.

Up we went at the first time of asking. When one considers how very few clubs do actually achieve this – as well as those who slide closer to the trapdoor at the other end of the league – Bruce and the club's leadership should be given due credit. All the same, he didn't last long. Defeat at home to the Villa (again) on Armistice

Day saw what was clearly a pre-arranged shuffle as he set off for Wigan and Blues lined up former Scotland manager, Alex McLeish.

McLeish, as every Blues fan supporter knows, went on to do what no other manager had ever done. There is, however, no statue of him adorning the forecourt at St Andrew's and nor is there ever likely to be.

Notwithstanding a spectacular win at White Hart Lane in his first game in charge, McLeish presided over two of the dullest, most tedious seasons imaginable. The first of these saw him oversee relegation in May 2008 and the second, promotion in May 2009. Yes, you did read that right. We were promoted in 2008/09 playing the deadliest, most pragmatic football known to man. By way of illustration, we finished second in the league scoring 54 goals in 46 games. Nine of those were scored by Kevin Phillips, including the coolest and most accomplished of finishes on the last day of the season at Reading, which sent us up and condemned them to the play-offs where they promptly lost to Burnley who were eventually promoted. As an interesting sidenote, Norwich and Southampton, neatly ensconced in the Premier League at the time of writing, were relegated to the third tier at the end of that same season.

Villa fans will have noted that I have skated over McLeish's first derby, but they will remember it with great relish. A 5-1 victory in these games will see you through your lifetime and that of your children. It was just one in a long line of no-shows that will always be the hallmark of McLeish's tenure. There was another just two weeks later when a completely shambolic display at Fulham saw them survive on 36 points and us go down with 35. It was just a taster for future debacles.

Those outside the Birmingham City bubble, and I suspect a fair few within it too, may regard this as too harsh a judgement. I apologise for any spoiler, but the next chapter is dedicated to the one genuine moment of success in our history and, probably, for some time to come. McLeish was the architect of that and the success was more creditable for the fact that it took place just as it was becoming plain to one and all that Carson Yeung was a fantasist and a charlatan. A broke fantasist and charlatan. What's more, McLeish oversaw our best run in the Premier League and, indeed, in the top flight in the modern era when, between November 2009 and January 2010, we went unbeaten in the league, acquiring 26 points from 12 games. At one point we won five games consecutively and from November onwards we were never in the bottom half of the table. You'd be forgiven for accusing me of being deliberately over-critical, especially given what you've gleaned of my relatively success-free history as a supporter. You could be right.

'The Invincibles' episode was peculiar inasmuch as we didn't quite know how to handle it. It made no difference whatsoever to matchday attitudes: a lifetime's habit of protecting yourself by starting off expecting the worst and then being happily surprised if it doesn't happen, is hard to break. But for a few weeks we churned out decent enough results. Once again, though, final figures may tell a story. In a 38-game season, we scored 38 goals – so, invincible or not, we were hardly scorching the earth with our performances.

During that heady invincible period, the starting 11 barely changed. Someone closer to the professional game at the top level may be able to cast more light on a suspicion that was frequently voiced among supporters at the time. While it's usually obvious that it is beneficial to keep a settled side when you're doing well, it was noticeable that the 'strains' and 'niggles' of which we are usually kept informed on a weekly basis seemed to have disappeared. Just saying.

When the unbeaten run ended with defeat in January by Chelsea, who went on to win the league, the rest of the season dribbled away with us gleaning a point a game and a ninth-place finish. Even as I write it, I concede that I should have been delighted with such fare, but there was a prevailing sentiment that we should have done so much better. As a cruel aside, 31 points would have been enough for survival that season – further proof of the 40-point myth. And in terms of not doing ourselves justice, it was against one of the hapless relegation saps that we fouled up once again.

Portsmouth eventually finished the season bottom of the league with 19 points. We played them in the last eight of the FA Cup in early March 2010 and in the week before we did so, they went into administration and began slithering towards the fourth tier of English football. We were eighth in the league and despite the unbeaten run coming to an end, playing with our usual uninspiring efficiency.

It's true that after a particularly leaden performance and the gift of two goals we didn't deserve much, but the game – from our point of view – hinged on an error on the part of the officials that modern technology in its acceptable form of goal-line alerts would have spotted immediately. At 2-0 down and with enough time left to make a go of it, a header from Liam Ridgewell snuck in at the post in the goal in front of the Blues fans. England goalkeeper, David James, scooped it out and looked hopefully, and guiltily, across at the linesman as we celebrated the goal. That wasn't given. How much difference it would have made can only be speculation. The report of the game on the BBC website made much of the fact that Birmingham would have an early chance of revenge in the same fixture in the league later that week and that it would be a chance for McLeish's men to continue their push for European football.

With typical Birmingham City perversity, we did indeed trudge down to Fratton Park again three days later and we did win and it looked as though we would keep pressing for our place in Europe. We then gathered a huge six points from our remaining ten games and looked more likely to be playing games on Saturn than in Europe. A promising season, our best in terms of league position since 1956, fizzled away into anonymity.

The next season, we did go to Europe. But this is Birmingham City and so, inevitably, there was a price to pay.

Chapter 10

We sing 'Oh, Nikola Žigić' to the tune of 'Seven Nation Army' by the White Stripes. Sometimes

I NEED to look deep into my soul and ask myself why the only player to warrant naming in a chapter title is Nikola Žigić. Especially as he was, and I'm being generous here, a touch limited.

Žigić was a Serbian international acquired by us from Valencia prior to the start of the 2010/11 season. He was 6ft 7in tall and, from time to time, looked reasonably coordinated. No commentator, however, ever wheeled out the cliché of him having a surprisingly good touch for a big man. To be honest, on his worst days – and there were a few – he looked like the bloke from the rugby team brought along to your game by a mate and then, with you a man short, being asked to stick himself up front and make a nuisance of himself. And yet on his best days, he was devastating and scared the opposition to death. This happened less frequently but, crucially, on a few big, big occasions.

Žigić played 137 games for Blues and scored 32 goals. When he left the club, he was reputed to be on £65,000 a week and by then he was playing for a team bumping around the second tier of English football. Quite how the club had entangled itself in such a bewildering web is a subject for a different kind of book (Daniel Ivery's *Haircuts and League Cups* unpicks it all in detail) but nothing seemed to sum up the capacity of Birmingham City to invent different routes to failure and institutional incompetence than this ridiculously inflated wage. But for a short period and in inspirational flashes, he was, as befits his looming physical presence, totemic.

Žigić came on as a substitute in the first game of the season at Sunderland (a 2-2 draw) and was a permanent fixture in the side thereafter. McLeish's style of managing his team had undergone no change. When, on 23 October 2010, Žigić sealed a 2-0 win over Blackpool, it was the first time we had won by more than one goal in the league since April in the previous year. Think about that for a moment. For 18 months – that includes one whole season, including the 'invincible' episode – there was never one period in a game when, even if we were winning, it was possible to relax and enjoy the final ten or 15 minutes. That can seriously colour your attitude, especially given a propensity to seek out disaster when none threatens – something we did with great aplomb in 2010/11. It was also a feat unrepeated for another six months and, typically, it did us no good in the long term.

We stumbled along in the autumn and early winter of that season and stopped the rot against the Villa with a goalless draw at their place in October. It was all dull stuff, but just enough to keep us out of the bottom three for most of the time. A 1-0 home win over defending champions Chelsea, thanks largely to their own wastefulness and a colossal performance from on-loan keeper Ben Foster, took us to the heights of 13th, which was as good as it got. But in the background, something else was going on.

In the League Cup we had bumbled our way to victories in the early rounds against Rochdale and franchise-football team, MK Dons. In a home tie against Brentford, then in the third tier of English football, we needed a 92nd-minute equaliser from Kevin Phillips to see the game go to penalties, which had been Brentford's route to victory over Premier League Everton in the previous round. On this occasion, however, Blues prevailed for an undeserved victory which saw us through to the last eight of the competition and … a home tie against the Villa.

After the shenanigans of the 2002/03 season, West Midlands Police had ensured that all Blues–Villa games were played as early as feasible on a Sunday morning. Along with many people, I had always assumed that this was to prevent alcoholic excess, especially during the hours of darkness, spicing up what was already a fiery situation. I have since been told that this may have something to do with police availability on a Sunday. On this occasion, however, they had few options but to do the best they could and so, on the first day of December, with snow already falling at the start of what would become a severe winter, the Villa crossed the city for a cup derby.

Under the lights, in the snow, against the Villa. Thunderous tackles on both sides, the ground full to the rafters. And in the centre of their defence, an ageing Richard Dunne up against the twisted legs of Nikola Žigić. Dunne played a blinder for us that evening. After 12 minutes he flannelled around a bouncing ball in the Villa penalty area, resulting in a spot kick for us. We had not had a penalty in the league all season – figure it out – and the only one to be scored outside of a shootout was by James McFadden in an earlier cup round against Rochdale – and he wasn't playing that evening. Neither was Kevin Phillips, the obvious candidate in such circumstances. Step forward Seb Larsson to put an indifferent effort past Friedel.

Plenty happened from then on in. Another goal-line decision went against us with the TV clearly showing the ball across the line. Žigić missed a sitter and Jerome, through one-one-one, was unable to keep his composure as he had on that famous afternoon at Molineux. And then, inevitably, Gabby Agbonlahor equalised for them. Inevitably because he made a habit of it right up until April 2017 when he waddled off the bench, looking as though he'd been existing on nothing but chips and gravy for two years, to score the winner in the 86th minute and make our survival in the Second Division look even less likely.

A word, then, about Agbonlahor. First, he was subjected to one of the few chants that I could not bring myself to either sanction or even grin ruefully about. It doesn't take much working out; it involves the last syllable of his surname and his mother. Unsurprisingly – and justifiably – he made great play of the tiresome gesture of cocking his ear to Blues fans on those occasions when he scored against us. The chant was even more pointed given a rocky relationship with his mother which had somehow found its way into the public domain. He was a Birmingham boy with deep-rooted Villa affiliations, so the disapproval heaped upon him was even more vitriolic. In the future, the same opprobrium would be levelled against another Villa local, Jack Grealish, with shameful and embarrassing consequences for Birmingham City and its supporters.

On the field that night, playing for Birmingham City, was Craig Gardner. He had started his career as a boy with the Villa. He played for them on 59 occasions from 2005 and then came to Blues in January 2010 – claiming that he was a lifelong Bluenose. Mmmm. In

October 2016 his younger brother, Gary, scored for the Villa against Blues in a 1-1 draw at St Andrew's and ran the length of the field to celebrate with their fans. He's now playing for the Blues and he says he's a lifelong Blues fan too. Given that other Blues fans have enjoyed scoring against us and made no secret of loving the moment – the irrepressible Troy Deeney springs immediately to mind – it may be too much to read anything into this. But Agbonlahor and, latterly, Grealish, are real-deal Villa and they have relished their successes against us – and as irritating as I find it, quite rightly too.

I had spent a good deal of the evening berating Žigić. I did this quite often and it usually took the form of one of these outbursts: 'Žigić, jump, you lazy bastard'; 'Žigić, get yourself into the penalty area, you lazy bastard'; 'Žigić, track him back, you lazy bastard'. You may have detected a pattern. On reflection I can concede how tedious this may have become for those around me and I recognise that someone somewhere may still be telling tales about the bloke behind them at St Andrew's who did nothing but get on Žigić's back all the time. I must have overstepped the mark at Forest's City Ground the following year because the bloke in front of me told me that if I didn't jolly well shut up, he'd punch my blooming lights out. That is, of course, an edited version. Words, but no fisticuffs, were exchanged but what was noticeable during this short-lived fracas was that opinion was divided as to whether my outpourings were fair comment or not. That's what Žigić did – he divided opinion. I kind of had the last laugh that day at Forest. Žigić was taken off after an hour when we were one down to be replaced by the dependable Chris Wood – turning out in the Premier League at the time of writing and scoring goals there – who scored twice to take us to an unlikely victory.

In the next seat to me that night for the Villa game was someone who was using his mate's season ticket. Fortunately, he also saw little to praise in Žigić's performance that evening and we both tutted along in gloomy agreement. Then, with four minutes left, tireless and trustworthy Cameron Jerome chased a lost cause of a hoof towards the corner of the Tilton End. Somehow, he managed to get it across the area and Žigić, falling over in a tangle with Richard Dunne, fluffed a shot which deflected off the grounded defender and over a flapping Brad Friedel.

In that barmy, ecstatic moment I turned to the stranger next to me – a bloke of about 40 – our eyes met in a moment of wonder and joy, mixed with mirth at the instant recognition that the lanky Serbian had had the last laugh on us and, reader, I hugged that stranger.

At the end of the game what seemed to have been a good-natured and celebratory pitch invasion by Blues fans turned into something a touch nastier as some made their way towards the Villa fans in the Railway End – now officially dubbed as the Gil Merrick Stand. As with our unloved cousins at Molineux, those responsible for seat allocations have engineered a built-in design fault about where away fans should be located. To be in the Steve Bull Stand at Wolves is to be the recipient not only of regulation, and entirely standard, verbal abuse but an occasional shower of cold tea, sprayed fizzy pop and other unmentionables. The same applies in the Gil Merrick.

With a few wannabe Zulus behind a wall of riot police, and others in the Gil Merrick Upper happy to share the dregs of their beverages with the Villa fans below – who, in their turn, were entertaining themselves by ripping up seats and setting off flares – it was quite a spectacle. Just for absolute clarity, I'll be careful what I say next lest I be accused of condoning any sort of violence at football matches or harking back to some daft notion of the good old days. But here goes … my current season ticket is in the Spion Kop. To my left, week in, week out, away supporters in the Gil Merrick churn out the same dull, repetitive and unoriginal repertoire of chants and songs to which dull, repetitive ripostes are intoned in return. Most weeks, it's just a silly ritual that goes no further. As I turn right out of the ground on my way out, the away supporters do the same from the adjacent gate and we mingle fleetingly before going our separate ways. But occasionally things are a touch spikier. When that happens, the constabulary is usually alert to it and will have formed a human barrier to keep supporters apart. What occurs afterwards is an embarrassment.

From behind the safety barrier of coppers, young men taunt each other and offer each other out. A braver set of boyos you've never seen. They do so from behind a wall of bored coppers in riot gear. It's a tedious bit of hooligan-like choreography performed, for the main part, by those whose physical bravery largely resides in their own heads. I know, at first hand, that real set-tos might well be taking place elsewhere, but those participants really don't want the intervention of an unwilling referee in the shape of police officers. Again, for the avoidance of doubt, I'm neither romanticising nor condoning such behaviour but it does, at least, seem to have the courage of its own convictions. A friend once accompanied me to a Blues game where the cowards' dance behind the coppers was taking place and expressed surprise at what he saw as a potentially violent and intimidating experience. To my shame, I found myself shrugging and telling him that it wasn't really anything and that if he wanted real football violence, he wasn't going to find it with a bunch of 17-year-olds prancing down the Coventry Road.

So, a little, mini riot-ette took place much to the great delight of the assembled media and a raft of commentators who took to the airwaves to fulminate and parade their common-sense credentials. As we listened to this on the radio in the car back south, the only voice of reason came quite late into the phone-in ranting and it was from an unlikely source. Local – and now national – radio broadcaster, Birmingham boy and

Albion supporter Adrian Goldberg piped up. A groan from those of us in the car. Another pontificating, condemnatory tirade from someone only too happy to have a pop at both of his local rivals. We were wrong. It's Blues vs Villa in a cup game, observed Goldberg. It's what happens. We'll all be at work tomorrow. Get over it. I've had a soft spot for him and his work since.

The two-legged semi-final was to be played against West Ham, with the first game at Upton Park. Žigić was only used as a late substitute in a game won by the home team, 2-1. Back at St Andrew's two weeks later, West Ham scored midway through the first half to give them a two-goal aggregate lead and it looked as though another set of dreams was about to be dashed. In one of those quirks of selection that bewilder fans everywhere, McLeish had once again decided not to start with Žigić but opted for the lightweight loanee, Matt Derbyshire – a player who obviously never felt at home with the club. At half-time, McLeish replaced him with Žigić who, from the very moment he entered the field of play, decided he was going to frighten the life and soul out of West Ham.

A corner from the right and, for once, the lazy bastard does jump, takes out two defenders by doing so and knocks it down for Lee Bowyer to slam a shot into the net. A corner from the left. West Ham won't get fooled again. Žigić is double-marked – and into the vacated space glides Roger Johnson to score an equaliser. In extra time, lifelong Blues fan Craig Gardner scores with a wonderful long-range shot and we are, indeed, going to Wembley. Not Cardiff. Not in the also-rans' cup final. To Wembley. To play the Arsenal.

I'm aware that any Birmingham (or Arsenal) fan reading this knows what happened on 27 February 2011, so I'll spare them – and all neutrals – a blow-by-blow account. The term 'underdog' does not even begin to cover our status on that cold February day. The Arsenal were in second place in the league with 56 points from 27 games; we were 16th with 30 points, having scored our usual parsimonious 25 from 26.

The story in short. Arsenal should have been down to ten men and a penalty awarded against them within the first five minutes. With true Elleray-style lack of nerve, referee Mike Dean failed to act when Lee Bowyer was brought down by Szczesny. But a tone was set by that early foray into opposition territory and somehow it seemed to convince the players, and us, that this might not be as straightforward as predicted. On 28 minutes we get a corner. The Arsenal marking is abysmal, Roger Johnson gets the first header and there, kind of jumping, is that lazy bastard Žigić to guide his header into the net. Is this really happening? Well, within ten minutes, normal service seemed to have resumed as van Persie equalised. That, we all assumed, was probably that.

Ben Foster made a number of wonderful saves and Blues defended, as they needed to, like men possessed. In between all of that, Keith Fahey, the man for whom the term 'unsung hero' might have been invented, hit the post, just to demonstrate that we weren't completely out of it. Niklas Bendtner, now back at his home club, came on for them in the 69th minute and, to our great delight, made no impression whatsoever. As in Cardiff ten years earlier, Blues began to look like the walking wounded and in the 83rd minute Fahey limped off to be replaced by Obafemi Martins.

For a bloke who has written himself into our history, Obafemi's career with us was fleeting. Had it not been for one moment in the late winter of 2011, you could have blinked and not even seen him.

He had been acquired on loan four weeks beforehand. He scored a good goal in the FA Cup against Sheffield Wednesday and then scored his goal at Wembley which, to be frank, if he'd missed, would have placed himself firmly in the history books as poor old Gordon Smith of 'and Smith must score' fame in 1983 (although, to be fair to Smith, the chance was not entirely straightforward). He played six games for us in all, but his name is still sung on a regular basis and probably will be until another unlikely moment of success ever comes along. One of the principal architects of the goal was Nicola Žigić. It was as basic as it was comical as it was unexpected and glorious.

A pump upfield from a Ben Foster free kick in our half. Žigić jumps enough to head it on but there's no one to pick up the flick for us … but right below us, at Wembley, Wojciech Szczesny and Laurent Koscielny do a little dance of hesitation and indecision and the ball pops out to Obafemi, six yards out in front of an entirely empty net.

At home games in recent seasons, and in common with most clubs, a collage of film clips of our most successful and treasured moments are played to stirring music before the teams come out. It's a device that is, after a while, met with the complete indifference born of familiarity. Three favourites, all referenced in this book, are there. Stern John in the last minute at Millwall from very close range; Stern John in the last minute against the Villa from very close range; Obafemi Martins in the last minute against the Arsenal from very close range. If, in a moment of idle diversion, I turn my attention to these episodes, my reaction is always the same: I think to myself that he's going to miss. Quite what the psychological process in play here might be is beyond me. I know exactly what happened. I was present and I saw it for myself. Yet somewhere deep in the unfathomable recesses of my consciousness, I am expecting the worst. I'm attempting no amateur psychoanalysis, but in my defence, I do know there are others who think the same. We can only be causes lost to sensible humanity, I suppose.

He doesn't miss. He puts the ball into an empty net. I hug my son, I hug the blokes around me, all of whom I know, as the London Supporters' Club has a block of tickets together – although I ensure that I am some distance from one of our number to whom modern standards of physical hygiene remain something of a mystery. We then fret for the remaining minutes of the game as Blues manage to hold on to win a cup. At Wembley, on the telly, against a top side. For the next half hour we sing, shake our heads in disbelief, cheer as the cup is held aloft and have to sit down to catch our breath occasionally. We have, as must always be the case, the stadium to ourselves; the Arsenal fans had departed on the final whistle – no staying behind to give their boys an appreciative ovation for their efforts. If it had been the gladiatorial arena, it'd have been thumbs down for Wenger and his stars.

Eventually we leave the stadium and a strange thing happens. As we walk back up Wembley Way to the tube, looking forward to a few more beers, it's quiet. We're sung out and wrung out. We're not dancing in the streets, we're just knackered. And, of course, we are unversed in this: what exactly are you supposed to do when you actually do win something? It would be inaccurate to call it anti-climactic as the warm glow of success is all-pervasive; it's just for that 20 minutes or so, there is an odd calm and maybe a quiet contemplation about how very, very good it will be to go into work or school tomorrow.

This last thought is very much in the forefront of my own mind – I know and work with plenty of Arsenal supporters. They all knew they were going to win and so did I. This is going to be glorious – and, all too temporarily, it was. The game must also have had a deleterious effect on Wenger and his team. In their remaining 11 games they collected only 11 points to slip from second to an eventual fourth. Eleven points: if only.

And a word or two about Wenger with whom, as Blues fans, we felt we had unfinished business dating back to February 2008. A few minutes into our home game with the Arsenal, Birmingham defender Martin Taylor went clumsily, but not maliciously or dangerously, into a tackle with Eduardo. The outcome was horrific. Players could not bring themselves to look at the resultant injury and there seems to be little doubt, given Arsenal's subsequent performance in that game, that the incident affected them deeply. Referee Mike Dean sent Taylor off which might have been an understandable decision in the heat of a very emotional moment, but looked at objectively, was probably harsh. The game finished 2-2 thanks to a last-minute Blues penalty and is also notable for the tantrum thrown by the Arsenal captain, William Gallas, at the final whistle. A graceless piece of conduct outshone only by the crass behaviour of his manager.

Arsène Wenger has often been described as 'professorial', principally on the strength of the fact that he wears spectacles. While it's true that he brought many beneficial innovations to the English game, for a bloke of obvious intelligence, he let himself down time and again with his post-match interviews. His insistence on occasional, selective blindness became genuinely comical. There was, however, nothing remotely comedic about his response to Martin Taylor's genuine error. In calling for him to be banned for life, Wenger opined that 'people will say that he's not the kind of guy who does that. But it is like a guy who kills only once in his life. There is still a dead person.'

Very classy, Arsène. You might have taken a leaf out of Eduardo's book when he summed up the incident by musing that 'shit happens'. If it was possible to do so, making Wenger squirm a little made the win at Wembley even sweeter.

For once, it did look as though it may well be a season when 40 points, possibly one or two more, might be required for survival. All the same, coming off the cup final, we already had 30 with another 12 games to go. There was a slight worry because seven of these were away from home and two of them were against Liverpool and Chelsea, but all of our home games were against teams in the bottom half and all the relegation candidates were destined to take points off each other. I'm sure that you've already detected the warped logic of the one-eyed supporter, all of which turned out, with grim inevitability, to end in misery and disappointment.

The signs seemed to be there on the Saturday after Wembley when we played the Albion at home and lost 3-1. Cup hangover. But that's kind of inevitable. We'll be fine. We scrape a draw away at Everton and lose carelessly away to relegation rivals Wigan and slip to

19th out of 20. And then, we seem to get the job done. Seven points from three games in early April leaves us in 14th with 38 points and six games to play. We might just need three, possibly even four, from these six games … in which we go on to score four goals, concede 15 and acquire one solitary point, finishing on 39 and so go down, once again, to the second tier. Two home performances of absolutely staggering ineptitude – and, don't forget, we are a bunch of supporters who know staggering ineptitude when we see it – against Wolves and Fulham set the seal on this unhappy demise.

On the last day of the season, there was still something to play for. If we could win at Spurs (yes, I did write that) we'd be fine. If Wolves lost by two clear goals to Blackburn and we drew, we'd be fine. If Wigan lost and Blackpool lost, we'd be fine as well. Even if we lost … and even as I type this – and as the next chapter will expand on this thought – I ask myself this question. I know there are a few candidates, but is there any set of supporters anywhere, probably in the world, who have had to undergo this convoluted set of potential outcomes prior to the last day of the season more often than us? Particularly in terms of possible relegation?

By 22 May 2011 we were a long way from my first forays to watch the Blues in the early 60s when you had to find the person with the transistor radio glued to his (it was always his) ear. For many years, and until very recently, TV coverage of anxious last-day crowds always managed to seek out one such relic from a bygone era, but phones and, on that day at White Hart Lane, the electronic scoreboard, kept us all up to speed. For a few brief moments late in the second half, we looked as though we might be OK. We'd drawn level with Spurs with another terrific strike from Craig Gardner, Wolves were three down to Blackburn and Wigan were only drawing at Stoke. Within minutes, it all turned to dust.

Wigan scored. Wolves scored twice. We now needed a winner. The story goes that as Blues pushed for that necessary goal, loveable 'Arry, the Spurs manager, unaware that goal difference had now come into play, asked McLeish what he was playing at by ploughing players forward, telling him that he only needed a draw. 'Arry's accountancy skills and grasp of basic arithmetic were on full show – something with which we were to become acquainted at first hand ourselves a few years on. As we pressed up the field, Spurs broke away and scored and that was that.

Twenty-six days later, McLeish, to universal astonishment and some mirth, took up a new managerial position at ... Aston Villa. It genuinely was a case of not knowing whether to laugh or cry. He had guided us to our one major trophy (it really is a bit much to bracket the 2011 win with that of 1963) but had then so mismanaged us from that point that we fell from a position of security to abject surrender. At all times our football had been dour and pragmatic, which was tolerable as long as results came our way, but at others was just blain boring. It must remain a source of some displeasure to him, as inured as he must be to the shifting loyalties and affections of football and its supporters, that he is not remembered with more affection than he is – although he must have known that moving over the expressway wasn't going to make him top of anyone's Christmas card list. To be fair to him, he did set the Villa off on a miserable run of seasons, culminating – long after he had departed – with their relegation in 2016. In his one season in charge they finished in 16th place and stayed up with – yes, you guessed it – 38 points.

The admirable Chris Hughton took over at Blues in a development that was met with optimism and enthusiasm. The fly in the ointment, however, was that Carson Yeung and his advisers, showing all the financial aplomb that landed him in a Hong Kong lock-up, had failed to make the usual arrangements and adjustments to players' contracts and wages in the event of relegation. Of these miscalculations, the most egregious was rumoured to be that a tall Serbian remained on the books at around £60,000 per week. On 27 February he had scored the goal that took us to short-lived glory. He didn't score again all season.

Oh, Nikola Žigić.

Chapter 11

We go to Europe and break a record

HERE'S A funny thing. As I'm writing this, the country remains in a complete dither about what to do about its relationship with Europe. If, by some freakish chance, this has been resolved by the time of publication, I can only imagine it will have been more by luck than judgement, or that the rest of the continent will have become so utterly bored and frustrated with us that it will have imposed a complete embargo on all trade, travel and social association. Conversely, football and its supporters have, after a rocky start, always wanted to be in Europe. And at the start of the 2011 season, notwithstanding our demotion, we were going there thanks to our League Cup win.

As for that rocky start, much of it was to do with our chums up the road in Wolverhampton, although we, too, played a part in putting football on the map in Europe – because that, in the misplaced vanity of the age, is what many people thought 'we' were doing. Although England had lost 1-0 to the USA in the 1950 World Cup, it was a result that could be put down to one of those freakish things with which sport can delight us. We were still the founding fathers of the beautiful game. What happened three years later, however, was something of a very different order.

First, Hungary's national team came to play England at Wembley; more unfortunate backwoodsmen coming to be taught a lesson. They won 6-3 and astonished those who saw it by both their skill on the ball and the flexibility of their tactics. Well, Johnny Foreigner may have foxed us once, but we'd never fall for it again. All that circus trickery might bamboozle a chap if he were caught off guard, but when England set off to Budapest for revenge in May 1954 those magical Magyars were in for a surprise.

Hungary 7, England 1. Maybe they did know how to play after all.

Before we come to Wolves's part in all of this, there is an unfortunate Birmingham City element to this episode. We supply very few England internationals at Blues. Since I first went in 1963 you can count them on the fingers of one hand and have a digit to spare. With one exception, since the war only Trevor Francis has hit double figures in terms of appearances. Bob Latchford scored a few times for England after he'd left us and Matthew Upson did so once. Trevor was the only one who scored a goal for England when actually playing for us. One of the reasons for this lack of goalscoring is that the only other England regular was a goalkeeper and he won all of his 23 caps when playing for Blues. What's more, he gained them all when playing for us in the Second Division. His name was Gil Merrick and he was between the sticks when Hungary put a combined total of 13 goals past England in two games in the early 1950s. To be honest, it's something to keep quiet about when it comes to looking at our record of supplying international players.

Undeterred by this Hungarian battering, league champions Wolves, with their fancy floodlights costing more than £30,000, laid down a challenge to the champions of Hungary, Honved, in what was the first move towards persuading the firmly conservative footballing powers that a competition between European clubs might be an exciting new development for the game. In a match at Molineux on 13 December 1954, Wolves beat Honved 3-2 and in an act that was staggeringly vainglorious, nominated themselves as champions of Europe. A story went the rounds that Wolves manager Stan Cullis, who would later come across the Black Country to take charge at Blues, had ordered excessive watering of the pitch at half-time to curtail the swift passing of the opposition that was flummoxing his players. If true, it's a telling metaphor about an attitude that stunted the progress of the game in this country for much of the time that followed.

All the same, the European *chat* was well and truly out of the *sac* and by a peculiar twist of circumstances, Blues found themselves in a pioneering role. A competition was established to coincide with European Trade Fairs and the principal cities involved in them. In the first of these, following Wolves's early foray, a London XI, comprising players from a variety of clubs from the capital, represented England. As the competition developed, largely unloved and unnoticed in the days of very sparse TV coverage, the opportunity came for Birmingham to be represented. I have been unable to uncover anything like a convincing narrative about why there was not a combined team from Blues, Villa and the Albion – with, one imagines, a token Walsall representative – but what emerged was that Birmingham City became plain Birmingham and in the 1960 'final' of the European Inter-Cities Fairs Cup, played over two legs in the spring of that year, met the mighty Barcelona. 40,524 people witnessed a goalless draw at St Andrew's on a pitch the likes of which we just don't see any more. It is a game of which there is surprisingly extensive footage to enjoy.

Six weeks later, the return fixture was played. The record shows a suspiciously neat number of 70,000 spectators present to watch the home side run out 4-1 winners, but ... if you visit, as any self-respecting football supporter must, the excellent museum at the Camp Nou, there, tucked away in one of the exhibitions, is a pennant commemorating the visit of Birmingham City on 4 May 1960. It doesn't take much of an imagination to picture the bafflement of visitors from around the world as their perusal of this great club's history is interrupted by some daft old Brummie calling out in glee in front of one of the more nondescript exhibits – 'Here! We're here! This is us. Here.' If you're a supporter, you'll understand.

Whether or not there was any money to be made in the Fairs Cup – which was the forerunner of the UEFA Cup, the third-tier European tournament – we entered it again in the following year and played Roma. The gloss may have worn off because only 22,000 (again, a rather over-exact figure) saw a 2-2 draw at home prior to a 2-0 defeat in Rome (60,000). So, to return to something mentioned earlier about money to be won in pub quizzes – 'Who was the first English team to play in a European competition final?' You'd be unlucky not to win the points on that one.

These early excursions, despite going relatively unacknowledged in the wider football world, did at least have some semblance of purpose and had been conceived as part of a wider strategy to develop the game and its competitions. The same could never be said of our only other participation in European football prior to 2011 – the colossally stupid and ill-fated Anglo-Italian Cup. Stumbling along unfeasibly from 1970 until 1996, 37 English clubs have found themselves duped into playing in this barmy farce which has become a byword for incompetent organisation and random, spectacular violence on and off the field of play. From Port Vale to Manchester United, supporters vie for the most freakish tale of the unpredictability and lunacy of this most bonkers of enterprises. We played in it on four occasions; once in 1972 and then, largely under the almost watchful eye of mad Barry Fry, three times between 1992 and 1996. One occasion has inscribed itself in our history: the Battle of Ancona.

For accuracy, I'll be clear – I wasn't there. In fact, 'only' 92 hardy souls made it over to Italy on 15 November 1995 as part of a crowd of some 800 (no, I haven't missed out any zeros). One of those 92 was my principal travelling companion and, to be frank, he has no more idea of what occurred off the pitch than anyone else, with the possible exception of the excellent Birmingham journalist Colin Tattum – Tatts. Events on the field of play were more obvious, but very ugly. I can't possibly outdo Rob Doolan's excellent account which you can google and enjoy for yourself, but after 90 minutes of kicking, punching and spitting, involving players, referee and managers, it all got even worse in the tunnel after the game. Rob writes with supreme understatement that 'there is no reliable account of precisely what happened next' but we can get a flavour of the mayhem from the fact that police invaded the Birmingham dressing room, confiscated players' passports and deliberately delayed their departure home.

Criminal charges were instigated against some of the players and the possibility of extradition and imprisonment was not, apparently, fanciful. The accepted wisdom is that Karren Brady employed her connections and operational know-how to bury the situation. As Rob acknowledges, there is no possibility of a credible account ever coming to light. However, a Birmingham City side comprising Liam Daish, Paul Tait and Ricky Otto, managed by Barry Fry, on a jolly-up in Italy on a Tuesday night. What, as the cliché suggests, could possibly go wrong?

But by August 2011, these ventures in the Fairs and Anglo-Italian Cups were history. The former had undergone a further transition from the UEFA Cup and was now the Europa League – and we were in it. Fully televised, Thursday night, Channel 5. At the end of the wretchedness of the 2011 relegation debacle, most of us were unsure as to whether this was a genuine consolation. A return to the top division had to be the priority for new manager, Chris Hughton. Was he even going to take the competition seriously or regard it as an encumbrance?

In the 2011/12 season, Birmingham City played 62 games. I reckon I saw 38 of them live along with a fair number on the TV. Under Hughton's astute, calm and dignified leadership, I think I can state with iron certainty that every single game was taken seriously including, to our great collective joy, the Europa League. One random incident captures this joy perfectly.

One Saturday afternoon in October 2012 I was sitting in a pub in Waterloo, nursing a pint and watching the admirable Jeff Stelling deftly handling Sky's rolling scores programme. Spoiler alert – Blues didn't go up at the end of the 2011/12 season, despite having reached the play-off semi-finals. Hughton had, unsurprisingly, received a better offer from sensible, stable Norwich City and amid tales of financial catastrophe, Lee Clark took over as manager. I'll return to the weird and woeful ramifications of that apparently innocuous statement of fact in the next chapter. But on 27 October 2012, having been unable to go to watch us at pricey Leeds because of the prior social engagement that saw me happily ensconced in the Hole in the Wall, I sat on quiet tenterhooks waiting for news from Elland Road.

I was perched on the end of a table where three other blokes, all of whom knew each other, were similarly gawping at the screen. We drifted into conversation and it transpired that two of them supported Crystal Palace and the other, Millwall. Two of my companions – the Palace fans – were knowledgeable and well informed and asked about quite how we had managed to slide from the comfort of mid-table and cup winners to our current predicament. I gave them, I hope, as concise a summary as was possible and then mentioned that the one saving grace from the whole sorry business had been our European adventure. The details wouldn't have been of interest to them and I didn't attempt to bore them with the minutiae of our Thursday night escapades. I just said that I had never, even in my wildest imaginations, thought I'd ever go abroad to watch the Blues in a meaningful competition. Having made my point, I returned my attention to the TV.

What happened next was pleasantly surprising and worth citing in its full vulgarity. 'I would fucking love to see Palace in Europe,' exclaimed one of my new companions. 'All these big fucking clubs saying they're bored with it – they want to think of their fucking fans.' And so on, with continuing profanity and to the clear approval of his mates. The Millwall fan had been around for a brief, and unpleasant, taste in 2004 as defeated FA Cup finalists in a year when Manchester United didn't need to be involved in such a lowly European level, and so had some quiet appreciation. My new Palace chum, though, was on a roll: 'You've been lucky, mate. I'd have bloody loved that.' He was right on all counts. It had been a gas.

For the record, because I just know you are interested, Blues won 1-0 at Leeds, Palace lost 2-1 away at Leicester and Millwall won 4-0 at home to Huddersfield – all results in the same division. As a further footnote, I had been at Millwall the previous Tuesday where they had gone into a 3-0 lead only for us to share the points by scoring three of our own. My new drinking companion had not been there or at either of the fateful Ferencvaros games in 2004 so I think it's fair to say that he was far from hardcore. As I have observed previously, I can only wonder at my capacity for recalling such detail when it often takes me all my mental prowess to remember why I've gone upstairs.

So, yes, it was taken seriously and it provided many of us with some of our best Blues-supporting memories, especially away from home and especially ... and, Blues fans, you know where I'm going here ... that night in Bruges.

There is a tendency in all walks of life for people to be a little careless about claiming attendance at major events. If everyone had been to the final concerts or seminal events they claim they had attended, there would, for example, have been six million people at the Stones gig in Hyde Park in 1969 (I was there) and a similar number at the 2003 anti-war demo (I was there, even though the Blues were at home to the Albion – won 1-0, Horsfield). As far as the fixture against Club Bruges was concerned, the reverse is true. Whatever the official estimates of the number of Blues fans in Bruges on 20 October 2011, you can double it with confidence and then add some. Readers may have noted that the prevailing tone of this book as it charts the lows and lowers of Birmingham City can occasionally be somewhat downbeat. Not so here. That night in Bruges was what football fans live for.

Bruges is a club with solid European football heritage. By an odd coincidence I had once seen them in a live European game – the 1978 European Cup Final at Wembley against Liverpool – where they lost to a single Kenny Dalglish goal. By way of brief explanation, and as a further visit to a world we have completely left behind, I had rocked up to Wembley, a few miles from where I was living, on the evening of the game, gone to the box office and bought a ticket for a few quid to stand and endure the dreadful sight lines for which Wembley was notorious. Not a bad, impromptu evening out. There was no such spontaneity involved in October 2011. Tickets for away supporters were highly sought after and, in the true anarchy of such football away days, non-possession had proved absolutely no deterrent to travel for thousands of Blues fans.

The central square in Bruges that Thursday afternoon was a picture of happy pandemonium. There had been faint rumours of the local hoolies turning up to take on these notorious Zulu warriors, but any such potential derring-do would have been quelled by the sight of thousands of Brummies cheerfully drinking themselves into a stupor, bunting footballs about and clambering up any available statue or monument. It all remained very good-natured and even when the strange news filtered around that we'd better all get going on the two-mile trek to the ground because there was, to all intents and purposes, no public transport or taxis available, the jolly mood remained unpunctured. Quite how some of our number made it to the stadium, either because of excessive Leffe consumption or natural physical decrepitude, is an enduring mystery.

The official estimate is that 5,400 Blues fans were in Bruges that night – unofficially it seems to have been put at around 8,000. I have no way of verifying this one way or another, but with all the allocated seats in one entire end of the ground occupied, officials sensibly seemed to decide that opening up other free spaces in the stadium was the right thing to do. The effect on the atmosphere in the ground was astonishing. Music producer Phil Spector is acknowledged as the founder of the concept of the 'wall of sound'. The noise in the Jan Breydel Stadium may have lacked the beauty and finesse of the Ronettes belting out 'Be My Baby', but if you wanted sense-assaulting, unrelenting racket, it was there in bucketloads that night.

No English club had ever beaten Bruges at home in a European competition and so when they took the lead in the third minute of the game it looked as though we were in for a night of jollity but without any correspondent footballing success. After all, we were bumping along just below halfway in the second tier of English football with a threadbare squad and still reeling from an unnecessary relegation. The clouds of the financial cataclysm that would soon embrace the club for the next few years were assembling ominously on the horizon. Bruges were European regulars. They would play in Europe in each of the eight following seasons, five of them in the elite Champions League. We were having a bit of fun, but we were getting a reality check.

And then we equalised. There must be books out there on the psychology of football supporting which explains why, having spent 20 minutes convincing yourself we were never going to get anything here anyway, that one goal can immediately make you believe that, you know something, we could win this. As the game ran its course the general feeling was that we would settle happily for a draw and this was confirmed when, late on, a horrific injury to Blues centre-back Pablo Ibanez held the game up for about ten minutes. A draw here would be a commendable result and as sorry as we felt for poor Ibanez, could we just get him treated and off the pitch because by now we were wasting valuable drinking time.

In the very final moments, the 99th minute, time added on because of the injury, the ball found its way out to Marlon King on the Blues right in front of the ranks of the travelling fans. His cross was met by Chris Wood who turned it into the net with the unspectacular, efficient aplomb which currently characterises his finishing in the Premier League.

It is the job of the writer to convey pictures, events and atmosphere with words. This one's a challenge. To start with, this was no hugging-strangers moment because, in a reprise of the pre-Taylor footage of crowds surging down terraces when goals were scored, that's exactly what happened. Physical contact was confined to either holding on to the person in front of you or trying to hold up the one behind. The noise was all-consuming and almost primeval: on a personal level, I'm never quite sure what it is that I am screeching when we score important goals. Multiply this random clamour thousands of times, accompanied by flailing arms and legs, and you might get something of what it was like.

Somehow, we managed to make our way back to the city centre, by now miraculously cleared of the afternoon's mountain of drink-related debris. Mirage-like, a few buses had appeared as we walked back and on one of those I sat next to a friend whose teenage daughter asked him, 'Dad – what do you think was better? That or Wembley?' Like every Blues fan who was at both games, I often ponder that question, but in many ways, the answer is not the point. Within eight months we had enjoyed two monumental, indisputable achievements. When you're Birmingham City or, in the case of many of you reading this, a supporter of a perennial non-achiever, the very fact that you've got such a choice to make is as delicious as it is surprising. On a personal level, for what it's worth, Wembley every time.

Once back in town, drinking venues were sparse, presumably because the afternoon had boosted profits so plumply that proprietors were sitting with their feet up happily counting their Euros into tall piles. Nonetheless, a few bars remained open and so an honourable mention is due to the patron of the Café de Kuppe who smilingly allowed his staff to fleece us all until four in the morning. If you're still in the Bahamas enjoying a life of cocktails and dancing girls at our expense from that night/morning, good luck to you. You're a part of our history.

Blues acquired ten points from the six games in the group stages of the Europa League and, in an echo of our going down with 39, this would have been enough to proceed to the knockout stages in most seasons. However, some rather dodgy goings-on between Bruges and Maribor, with the latter losing at home to them having been three up, meant that a potential visit to Valencia – the mind does truly boggle – was denied us. It had been a brilliant venture and appeared to allow Hughton to build a team capable of mounting a serious promotion challenge. A brilliant run at the start of the new year saw us in third place by the end of February. In the middle of an unbroken run of 11 games from Boxing Day, that lazy bastard Žigić scored all four in a 4-1 victory at Leeds. He was instrumental in getting two Millwall players sent off at The New Den in a game in which he didn't score but which we won 6-0. These were good days.

By the end of March 2012 we were firmly cemented in the play-off places with no serious prospect of automatic promotion. So, off we went to the play-offs again and replicated our dismal failures of the Francis era, losing away and drawing at home to Blackpool. An immediate return to the top league was not achieved, which was the only possible route to redemption from the financial calamity that was about to engulf the club. Hughton had done us proud. He had built a side that had done well in Europe, had embarked on a good FA Cup run in which we had forced a replay after a draw at Stamford Bridge and had almost squeaked us back into the Premier League. We had nothing to really show for it all, but it had been a decent season. We waved him off to Norwich with a heavy, but grateful, heart.

Things weren't going to be as good for a very long time. Not nearly as good.

Chapter 12

Mayhem, the great escape and the man with the swivelling eyes

BLYTH SPARTANS play in the sixth tier of English football. At the time of writing, late autumn 2019, they are 21st in a 22-team division. It took them 13 games from the start of the season to register their first victory. They are managed by Lee Clark. It's entirely possible that Lee Clark is one of the nicest fellows you could wish to meet, but on the evidence of his public actions as a football manager, he is off-the-scale barking mad. For two seasons from 2012 to 2014, he managed Birmingham City.

It's entirely true that he managed Birmingham City when they were run by a cabal of people who generally displayed the business acumen of punters convinced that they could find the lady at a street-scammers stall

– and that part was not his fault. It's also true that when he came to us, he appeared to have done a half-decent job at Huddersfield Town, with a win rate of nearly 50 per cent and a side that was on the up. He might not have been completely barking: we might have turned him that way. It's possible – but unlikely.

He had played 440 games in the top flights of English football and had been on the verge of selection for the national side. He was a dynamic, forceful player, but there were signs that he might just not have been the brightest candle on the cake. He had played for much of his career at Newcastle before making a controversial move to their rivals at Sunderland. While under contract there, he was spotted at the 1999 FA Cup Final among Newcastle fans wearing a tee shirt insulting his current club – his employers – to the effect that they were 'sad Mackem bastards'. He always looked slightly distracted and when he took up his managerial role with us, he didn't seem to be able to look at anyone when being spoken to in post-match interviews. Frankly, that was only a minor consideration as whatever it was he had chosen to say was usually utterly incomprehensible.

Somehow, despite a dreadful start to the 2012/13 season, Clark steered us through to a respectable mid-table finish. When I say 'steered' I can only emphasise that I'm using the term in its loosest way. Seven games into the season in a match televised on a Saturday teatime, we were walloped at home 5-0 by Barnsley. By the end of the game it was glaringly apparent to those of us left in the ground that no single player had the faintest idea of where he was meant to be playing. It was the precursor of two years of such mind-blowing disorganisation that nothing, but nothing, in Lee Clark's selection decisions would have surprised anyone.

Fortunately, the club had managed to hold on to some stalwarts such as Curtis Davies and Steven Caldwell at the back and with Chris Burke supplying Marlon King and that lazy bastard, Žigić – nine goals in 23 appearances, 12 as sub and, somehow, getting himself sent off twice – we got through the season relatively unscathed. It didn't last.

We lost nine out of the first 14 league games in the following season, notwithstanding some eye-catching stuff from loanee and future England international, Jessie Lingard. Then a decent unbeaten run of ten games saw us in a relatively comfortable 17th place at the turn of the year. But whatever Santa had brought down the chimney in the Clark household had the effect of making his bizarre conduct even more outlandish. As travelling companions we would challenge each other to concoct the most unworkable combination of players, only for them to turn out to be alarmingly, and hilariously, accurate. Everyone has their own 'favourite' but it is generally accepted the line-up for the home game against Blackburn Rovers on Easter Monday 2014 hit an all-time high, or low, depending on how you looked at it. Just to be sure that this was not false memory, I double-checked the team and it is completely impossible to sort the names available into any workable combination. We were four down at half-time, managing to stem the tide to lose 4-2.

Clark became visibly more deranged with every passing day. A few weeks prior to the Blackburn lucky dip and on the back of a run of seven defeats in ten games, we salvaged a rare and precious point with a last-minute equaliser at home to Burnley. Dear old Lee expressed his glee or frustration or both by manically kicking seven shades of sunshine out of the advertising hoardings near the dugout. If we hadn't been worried beforehand, the signs were clear enough now. In the next nine games we won twice and lost the rest; we went to Bolton on the last day of the season with a realistic possibility that we were about to descend into the third tier of English football for the first time since 1995. I'll cut and paste most of that sentence because I'll be using it again soon.

Bolton. 3 May 2014. Midday kick-off. We need to do better than Doncaster Rovers, who are away at Leicester. At half-time, it is goalless in both games. We are going down. Just short of the hour, Lee Chung-yong scores for Bolton. It remains goalless at the Walkers Cheese and Onion Bowl. We are going down. But wait … a penalty for Leicester, which they score. If we can get an equaliser then, as things stand, we could just squeak it. And just as that thought takes root, Lukas Jutkiewicz – who later becomes a folk legend at St

Andrew's – makes it 2-0 to Bolton and we're sunk. There can't be any way back. We need something truly remarkable and heroic.

Step forward you useless, lazy, overpaid bastard. A magnificent cross from the left from Mitch Hancox and Žigić not only jumps, he soars, he hovers in the air and he plants a brilliant, unstoppable header into the corner of the net. Over at Leicester, where we are unloved as a club, this apparently prompts calls from the home supporters to let one in lest we score an equaliser. And we push like fury for just that. Still 1-0 at the Crisp Factory. In the 90th minute, a scramble in the Bolton goalmouth. The ball pops up to Žigić who, once again, plants a header firmly towards goal. It's in, isn't it? We're pre-goal-line technology and neither the referee nor linesman (you can call them assistant referees if you really must) indicate anything. The ball pops up and there is Paul Caddis. He's 5ft 7in tall.

I wrote earlier about my irrational concern when watching footage, years later, of so many of our last-minute dashes at either glory or salvation. I still watch, in the full knowledge of what actually happens, and I think he's going to miss. The same applies to this instance. Caddis's jump to get over the ball and head it downwards into the goal seems to me to be akin to those stories of people who, in moments of danger and crisis, find the momentary strength to lift burning iron girders to save their loved ones. No one remains still long enough to hug or be hugged. Doncaster have not equalised in the East Midlands and we are safe.

Down on the touchline Clark slaloms around like a whirling dervish, his eyes facing all points of the compass simultaneously. Up in the media centre, Colin Tattum, his voice clearly shaking with high emotion, intones that this great club must never, NEVER, find itself in this sort of situation again (oh, Tatts, if only you'd known then) and on the terraces the mayhem continues. For most Blues fans in the crowd at Bolton that day, the experience of escape was a relatively new one. If your first season of watching us dated way back, then memories of Trevor Smith bulldozing us to safety some 50 years earlier introduced a note of nostalgia to the whole episode.

Nikola Žigić never started a league game for Blues again. He had scored some of our most important goals during the period he played for us and it was most definitely not his fault that his agent had been astute enough to fleece our feckless owners for such an astronomical wage. As a Brummie who, like so many of my compatriots from the city, loves a moan, he provided a great target but can proudly proclaim that in an era where players come and go with dizzying rapidity, he made a mark and was unforgettable. The lazy bastard.

For all the euphoria of the moment, it was clear to everyone that this had to be the end for Lee Clark. For one thing, we had not won at home since 1 October.

Just to put some flesh on the bones of that statistic, parents had taken their child's expectant hand as they made their way to enjoy watching their team at home and for seven full months, they didn't win. Fourteen games, eight defeats, six draws. That's almost child abuse. With this dreadful home record, the jaw-dropping ineptitude that had seen us on the brink of the abyss along with Clark's embarrassing persona as the club's public representative, only one outcome was possible.

On 9 August 2014 a new-look Blues took to the field at Middlesbrough's soulless Riverside Stadium managed by … you'll be ahead of me here … Lee Clark. In a 2-0 defeat the players, many of whom were new to the club, gave the impression that they were unfamiliar with each other and there was certainly no discernible style of play. It was impossible to know whether this was part of a bedding-in process that might be expected or if it was just business as usual under the wayward eye of Lee Clark.

The following week we won at home and the hoodoo was broken. A clear and decisive style of play emerged with the players themselves showing confidence in each other and a certainty about their approach to the game. None of that is true. It was a shambolic, scraped 1-0 win over Brighton and in our next seven games we scratched together four points and slithered to 21st place in the table. On the last day of September, we won away at Millwall but that was not enough to save Clark. After another home defeat – to Bolton – he was sacked.

Readers will note, I hope, that I have tried to maintain an amused note when talking about him. He can only be held partially responsible for our comically inept demise. On a serious level, however, what happened to him next is alarming. Within weeks he was in post at Blackpool. In normal circumstances, there's nothing wrong with a bloke moving swiftly from one job to another. But even to an unpractised, lay eye, it was clear that Clark's mental health had taken a battering. It speaks ill of football's governing bodies, be it those charged with enforcing risible notions of financial fair play or identifying fit and proper persons, that no one from the League Managers' Association took him to one side and told him to give it a break for a while.

From Blackpool to Kilmarnock to Bury to Blyth. His win percentage never rising above 28 per cent. And still crazy after all these years. Look after yourself, Lee.

He had left the club in a much worse place than he had found it and most – but by no means all – of that was his fault. You could argue that what happened immediately after his departure was partially down to him, but events at St Andrew's on a Saturday in late October 2014 can only be attributed to deep and damaging structural deficiencies.

By now, attendances at St Andrew's, where expectations, even by Blues standards, were below basement level, had dropped to around 14,000. Fewer than that turned up to watch us play Bournemouth. Yes, that's Bournemouth, now firmly established in the big boys' league but who had spent most of their century-plus history bumbling around the bottom divisions, nearly going out of business completely six years earlier. By October 2014 some astute managerial actions at all levels saw them building the side that would win the league and get promoted, gathering 90 points and scoring 98 goals along the way. Eight of those 98 were scored at St Andrew's on a mild Saturday afternoon, just before the clocks went back. I only witnessed six of them. I'd managed to sit through all seven against Liverpool, but this was too much for me. As I slouched down the hill for a much-needed pint, I heard the hollow cheers from Bournemouth's fans echoing round the near-empty stadium I had abandoned. I know I've tried to reach out to all fans to share our common experience of misery and disappointment, but, really, 8-0. At home to a side in your division. Beat that.

Two days afterwards, Blues appointed Gary Rowett as manager. He had played for us 87 times between 1998 and 2000 and had been an impressive, adventurous right-back who fulfilled the essential criterion for Blues fans of demonstrably giving his all on the field of play. He'd done a two-year stint as manager at Burton Albion, getting them to the play-offs of the fourth tier twice where, despite reaching the final on one occasion, they failed to get promoted on either. The first thing to notice about Rowett was that he spoke well – notwithstanding a habit of th-fronting (pronouncing f for th) – which seemed to become an issue for some of the more small-minded of his detractors as his star waned for that minority. To be fair, Professor Stanley Unwin (younger readers will have to google him) would have sounded crystal clear after Lee Clark, but Rowett gave the immediate impression of being capable, thoughtful and sensible. He wore a V-necked sweater with more style than any one man should be capable of doing.

He inherited a side that was bottom but one of the Second Division who had just been eviscerated 8-0 at home. The next weekend that same side had to venture into inhospitable Staffordshire to play Wolves who had made a very good start to the season. Rowett set the stall out for his stewardship by drilling his players to get a 0-0 draw. It is impossible to overestimate the importance of that first step in setting the tone for some genuine belief – and relief – for a club existing on the bones of its arse.

In the 31 games for the rest of that season, we acquired 52 points and finished tenth in the table. Seven weeks after the humiliation of the 8-0, we put six of our own past Reading at home. Other than a 4-0 seeing-to by Derby at home on Boxing Day, there were no more excruciating humiliations and although the football was hardly scintillating, Rowett did the best that he could with the limited funds available to him by playing functional, pragmatic football. When he came on the radio to speak after games, his assessment generally accorded with what you'd seen yourself. He wasn't saintly; like most managers, he had the odd unjustified gripe and moan, but most of the time he spoke sense. It may seem to you that I might be overplaying the extent of his contribution to the club and that's possibly true. That's because what happened to him as time moved on, although I acknowledge a strain of belief different from my own, was mind-bogglingly stupid. And that's even by the high standards of Birmingham City and those who had appropriated it.

In the season that followed, Rowett continued in the same vein of unadventurous but efficient football. We spent most of the season between seventh and tenth place, where we eventually finished after a nondescript end to a season in which the play-offs were always just a touch out of reach. But who knew? Two solid tenth-place finishes and maybe, just on the off chance, we could be building a team and a set-up that could take that next step.

The start of the 2016/17 season mirrored practically every season in the Championship. Teams bundled together separated in such a way that two consecutive wins could see you rapidly ascend the table. Blues under Rowett continued to play steadily and efficiently and, indeed, a bit more so than usual. On the morning of 14 December I was pleased to wake up in Mumbai and hear that we'd won a scrappy game at home to Ipswich to put us in seventh place, out of the play-off places only on goal difference and just three points off third. Maybe this season. Who knew? I was less happy by the end of the day having watched a regulation England batting collapse and capitulation, but what happened some 48 hours later as I landed at Heathrow perplexed me even more. As I switched on my phone on landing, it went into overdrive.

This wasn't just my phone provider welcoming me home and thanking me for being dim enough to pay extortionate rates for using their services in foreign lands. The red heat from my phone was telling me that Rowett had been sacked, that new owners were about to install a manager of their choice and that bookies had stopped taking bets on Gianfranco Zola being that appointment. I'm prepared for supporters of other clubs to skip a paragraph or two while I address something of a domestic dispute.

Just before doing so, a general observation. Football now exists in its own spotlighted existence of 24-hour news, talk stations and tabloid scandals. If we're daft enough, and because it's so disproportionately and stupidly important to so many of us, we can convince ourselves that we 'know' the central personalities involved and that we 'know' what's happening at our club. On a personal level, I have never known anyone who has worked at a football club above the fifth tier and I haven't had many conversations with such people about what actually happens day to day, even at that level. My own life experiences have furnished me with a pretty good idea of what happens in a range of workplaces with which I've been familiar. None of these include a top-level professional club. Some journalists at the serious end of the business sometimes seem to have some insight, but in all honesty, they're dealing with a business that – even at the very top – often seems to be run as much by emotion as by financial acumen and considered forethought. I won't credit that dreadful genre of sporting 'biographies' – 'he was a great lad but a beggar with a drink in him – and he liked a few' – as shedding any light on the beautiful game.

All of which is by way of painting the backdrop for the reasons for Rowett's summary dismissal. Those 'in the know' accused him of being on the lookout for a new, better paid job and an unwillingness to commit entirely to the 'project' promised by the new owners. The selfish so-and-so. In an industry where employment is so secure and where capricious, vain owners are unknown; where loyalty is on display in all aspects of the business; where patience is a virtue seen everywhere, a young man, eager to build his career, keeps his eyes open for opportunities for personal advancement. Yep – let him rot. Him and his awful, turgid football and his tenth places.

Zola's first game was at home to Brighton. It was odd. As the teams came out there was no great fanfare, blasting the introduction of our new manager. It was as if those around the club could sense the suspicion of the fans about what was going on. All the same, as the game progressed we did just about OK against a side that finished in the top two with some ease at the end of the season. Zola had obviously told his players to be a little more expressive with the ball than under the previous manager. That might have worked if they'd been any good. Most of them weren't. One moment summed up all the worries and gave a precursor of the 21 games of gloom – which yielded 13 points – that were to follow under Zola.

Ryan Shotton is a decent football player. Like most of us who watch football who have played at mudbath level, he is a hundred times better than we have ever been, so to call him a trundling journeyman seems something of an insult – but that's what he is. He's notched up over 300 appearances, mostly around the second tier of English football and is a good, old-fashioned, no-frills defender. Under Rowett he confined himself to heading the ball away, kicking it into touch if needed and pulling off the last-minute tackles which always betrayed his less than perfect positional sense. He was a perfectly serviceable player and an obvious trier. When we'd played the newly relegated Villa in the league at St Andrew's a few weeks prior to Rowett's departure, he'd dyed his dreadlocks blue and that was generally received as a good thing. Ryan Shotton was OK.

A few minutes into our first game under Zola, he did something that had us all catching our breath. Receiving a pass from one of his full-backs in his own half, instead of looking for someone better to pass to, or hoofing up for Lukas Jutkiewicz to forlornly lumber after, he calmly stepped forward with the ball at his feet, got his head up and surveyed the scene around him as if pondering the possibilities offered to him by his alertly mobile team-mates.

For just a few moments, he must have convinced himself, possibly encouraged by Zola, that he was a reincarnation of Franz Beckenbauer, the Emperor, striding majestically forward before picking apart the most watertight of defences. A Brighton player approached Ryan and he hoofed it up to Jutkiewicz, but it was a telling moment. In a further omen for the future, we lost the game having been one up with eight minutes to go.

A few weeks later we lost 4-1 at home to QPR in the league. Our travelling group had gone to the game on the train and on the way home to London jostled for space with Chelsea fans, happily triumphant from a win at Wolves in the cup. A good deal of noise from an adjoining compartment revealed that Zola – properly revered by Chelsea fans – was also making his way back to the capital. We deliberated about whether to take the opportunity to share our opinion about his managerial capacities – at this point we had five points from 12 games under his leadership – but given that we were hugely outnumbered by adoring Chelsea supporters, decided it was prudent to remain unnoticed.

However, as we disembarked, the opportunity arose to have a quiet word with him and to politely express our dissatisfaction. He was properly apologetic and quietly courteous. And then he said this. 'The players. They're just not confident enough.' He was being hustled away and so there was no opportunity to take it any further. Nonetheless, it's an illuminating comment. Rowett – and later Monk – looked at the players available to them, slotted them into their best possible positions and limited their possibilities for causing major ricks. Zola wanted them to be like him and the players he had played with – and they just weren't good enough for that.

His brief, miserable tenure came to an end after a home defeat to Burton in April. We were 20th in the table, facing the drop yet again. We had three games to go to save ourselves. The first was against the Villa away. Harry Redknapp was appointed manager, our third that season.

Mayhem? Yep – that just about covers it. But more was to come.

Chapter 13

We discover that we were only previously close to mayhem

LOVEABLE 'ARRY. He went on the airwaves and declared us a 'proper football club'. He either knew, or had recently learnt, the words of 'Keep Right On' and he sung them. He promised he'd do his best to keep this famous football club up. Goodness only knows how much our loony owners were paying him. A few days after his appointment he was to take us to Villa Park. Villa's manager was now Steve Bruce and he knew a thing or two about this derby game. Above all, he knew that the very presence of Gabriel Agbonlahor would be worrisome to us all.

Agbonlahor was now significantly portlier than he had been in his prime and consequently had only started four games all season. Bruce stuck him on the bench where he kept him until the 59th minute, at which point the game was goalless. To accommodate his presence, Jack Grealish was substituted and was sportingly applauded from the field of play by Birmingham's supporters. Three minutes later Agbonlahor was booked for a tussle with Ryan Shotton and then, with weary predictability, he prodded the ball home when Blues failed to clear their lines. He had not been on the field for ten minutes. We huffed and puffed but to the glee of our neighbours, we achieved nothing. Two games to go, still deep in the mire.

Huddersfield Town, soon to be promoted via the play-offs, enflamed the ire of our relegation rivals by putting out a weakened side at St Andrew's a week later in a game which we won. Nevertheless, other results went against us and after two years of obscure mid-table comfort, we were back on familiar territory on the final day of the season. This entailed thinking of not just our own result, but that of others as well. We were away at Bristol City. Of the two sides in the swamp with us, Blackburn visited Brentford and Forest were at home to Ipswich. Maybe someone would do us a favour. As if.

If you've read the introduction to this book, the outcome will be known to you. A single goal from Che Adams in the first half just about secured our victory but our survival was, once again, in jeopardy until the very final second of the game. Blackburn and Forest were winning easily and a Bristol equaliser, to which they came perilously close, would have sent us down. At the final whistle, we hugged. For the second time in three years we had been made to wait until the very last moment of the very last game to ensure that we didn't slip into the chasm of the third tier. If Tatts went on local TV and radio to explode into a rant about this NEVER happening to this club again, I didn't hear it. Down on the touchline 'Arry merrily cavorted with his new charges and for a few moments we all allowed ourselves to forget that he was an unscrupulous rogue who had left assorted debris from the financial wreckage of his managerial career in his wake and had once, allegedly, opened a bank account in his dog's name.

On the radio home we heard him pledge his future to his new-found love and most of us shrugged and laughed. He had come for a payday, had achieved what he was employed to do and would now sail off into the footballing sunset, his reputation enhanced, his pockets bulging, our gratitude ringing in his ears and his folklore status cemented. It didn't quite work out like that.

Our owners fell for 'Arry's line hook, line and sinker. You'll have picked up by now that, broadly speaking, I haven't delved too far into the personalities and capabilities of those who have owned us since my first trudge up the Coventry Road in December 1963. I do know that their affection for, or knowledge about, Birmingham or Birmingham City ranges from scant, to limited to non-existent. I am not one of those who demands that they spend their money on something I happen to like, but that doesn't stop me expressing complete astonishment at their lack of knowledge, vision or imagination. Their shortcomings as a species are exposed much more forensically elsewhere – on a local level by Daniel Ivery and nationally by the tenacious David Conn. Our dithery lot fell for Redknapp's spiel as did the thousands who bought season tickets in the hope of the new dawn he was about to bring. They also gave him money. Lots of it. What could they have been thinking?

Rumour – and that's all it was – had it that 'Arry was in infrequent attendance at a chaotic pre-season. He brought in lots of players – three of them from Brentford – for undisclosed fees and hiked up the wage bill. He bought Chiekh Ndoye from French club, Angers. My own playing 'career' was at the lowest levels but I do know that I have played with better players than Chiekh Ndoye. He and his agent must have a gold-framed picture of 'Arry adorning their palatial residences as they count their money and wonder at their astonishing good luck. Eight games into Redknapp's period of office, we had four points. After a fifth consecutive defeat at the hands of Preston at home, his connection with the club was severed. Why he hadn't walked away a hero that day at Ashton Gate is difficult to fathom. In the meantime, he had punched a whacking great hole into what was already a precarious financial set-up. And we kind of knew it wasn't going to get any better.

Steve Cotterill, whose reputation as a behind-the-scenes coach had been well established at a number of mid-ranking clubs, including ours, took over as manager. The one thing to say about this is cruel but fair: as supporters we had, at least, been made familiar with what a man out of his depth with no obvious capacity to swim to safety looked like. Readers old enough to be familiar with Premium Bonds will know that the winning numbers were generated by a machine called ERNIE – the Electronic Random Number Indicator Equipment. It was the firm belief of some of us that a similar device had been installed in the dressing rooms at St Andrew's and that Cotterill, like one of his predecessors, Lee Clark, tumbled the names of his squad into this apparatus and out came a team of players, haphazardly selected and placed into a pre-set formation. That suspicion makes just as much sense as some of the teams that both of them put out.

Cotterill took over a team in 23rd place and left it 24 games later in 22nd. We had at least managed a few home wins but for the second season running, and for the third time in five years, we were in clear danger of relegation. On 4 March the owners appointed Garry Monk as manager – our fifth permanent manager in 18 months. If this was to be the harbinger of salvation, it didn't start well as he lost his first two games, keeping us solidly rooted in 22nd place.

Eventually, under Monk's management we eked out a few decent results and there were even signs that there might just be a sensible style of play emerging. None of which prevented the inevitable. As results unfolded, it all came down, as we kind of knew it would, to the last game of the season.

On 6 May 2018 I had a couple of pints and trod the beaten path I had first taken some 55 years earlier. By my reckoning, this was the 11th time during that period that our fate – promotion or relegation – came down to what happened on the last day of the season. That's not counting five play-off attempts and those occasions, too numerous even for me to bother calculating, where we may have secured our fate as early as the penultimate game. Three of those last-day instances had crammed themselves into the five previous seasons; no one could ever call it boring, but it was losing its sheen as a thrilling event. Looking at our record during those six decades, reproduced as an appendix for those of you who like such trivia (that'd be me too), there do seem to be plenty of mid to lower finishes. Apart from the relief of Rowett's dull tenth places, most of them fail to register much in the memory – so maybe end-of-season unease isn't such a bad thing after all.

We were playing Fulham who, in recent seasons, had made a habit of destroying our survival hopes, albeit in the Premier League. For those of us with longer memories, the Maine Road disaster that denied us a cup final place in 1975 also loomed large. A draw would almost certainly have been good enough, but Fulham needed a win to keep alive any hope of automatic promotion. On a bright, sunlit Sunday afternoon at St Andrew's, Blues turned in a quite stunning performance to ensure our survival once again. No goalkeepers were bundled into the net at any point. At 2-0 with six minutes to go, Fulham scored to give them faint hope and us a few moments of apprehension, but almost immediately a Blues break ended with a Che Adams goal and we were able to enjoy the last knockings of the season – a luxurious treat in comparison with the last-moment jangling of previous seasons. Fulham went into the play-offs and were promoted, beating the Villa in the final, so all's well that ends well.

A word is needed about two of these last-ditch escapes. In 2014, we escaped with 44 points, in 2018 with 46. In most seasons in the second tier, this would not have been enough by some distance. In 2013, to our great delight, Wolves went down with 51 and with that they disappeared into footballing oblivion forever. Well, that's if you forget their current status in the upper reaches of the Premier League, of course. I include these numbers as a counterbalance to the gripe earlier about the number of points that saw us drop from the top level in 2011. Fairness and impartiality are not part of the natural make-up of the committed supporter, but it would have been a touch one-eyed not to have recognised this morsel of good fortune.

I'd like to be able to report that even by the high standards set for ourselves in terms of self-generated drama, that that was it for a while. And that's almost true. After a slightly disappointing start to the 2018/19 season in which results didn't reflect the level of our performance, Monk instilled a decent system built around a couple of good players and by the end of February we were sitting happily in the top half of the table. A reasonable run could even see an unlikely tilt at the play-offs. Readers who have been paying attention to the pattern of how the fates treat Birmingham City will know that such a run did not materialise. What's worse, March 2019 proved to be an eminently discreditable and embarrassing chapter in our history. A *mensis* truly *horribilis*.

On 2 March we were in eighth place in the table. By 29 March we were 18th. We had lost five games in a row, been the subject of national opprobrium because of the conduct of one of our supporters and been deducted nine points as a penalty for the financial misdemeanours that had characterised the complete incompetence and probable dishonesty of those charged with keeping the club's affairs in order. Throughout this book, I've played on the common trope of 'only at ... (insert your club here)', but there must be something remotely unique about this. From potential play-offs to potential relegation within days. That was new, even for us.

I'm not going to dwell on the incident at St Andrew's on 10 March when a knuckle-headed Blues supporter inscribed his five minutes of infamy on our history by his limp-wristed flap at Villa's Jack Grealish. It was an act of breathtaking stupidity and cowardice that affected the club, the supporters and the players and it is to the immense credit of the latter, along with the manager, that they picked themselves out of this slump and steered clear of any danger of relegation with relative ease. Whether or not it was instrumental in inspiring the Villa – above whom we had resided in the table for much of the season – to the startling run that ended in promotion via the play-offs is debatable. What it most definitely did was cast a pall over four weeks when it wasn't great to be a Blues supporter.

But Monk guided us clear of the potential danger with an unbeaten run of seven games as the season ended. Like Rowett, he continued to sound thoughtful, measured and sensible and most of us thought he'd done a pretty good job with the players at his disposal, particularly against the backdrop of the turmoil and speculation that culminated in the docking of nine hard-earned points. In which case, it's probably a mystery why it should have shocked any of us that he was sacked six weeks after the season ended.

We spent a good deal of the first decade of the 21st century in the top flight of English football, but as the end of the second decade approaches. It had been characterised by incompetent leadership along with vanity and carelessness on the part of our faceless owners – all of which have led to almost permanent flirtation with disaster. Why on earth any of us would expect anything different would be a triumph of hope over experience.

I've tried not to overdo reference to our wonderful anthem, 'Keep Right On'. Harry Lauder's original lyrics did not include the observation that we were 'often partisan' but his words have been altered and we've taken up the notion with all the grumpy, dog-in-the-manger stubbornness for which Brummies are renowned if not admired. It's a line often misheard: after a particularly raucous afternoon at Stamford Bridge, a young Chelsea steward politely asked me why we sang about being off to Pakistan. Another phrase is often blurred over in the singing. At the end of the road, we are promised that we'll come to our 'happy abode': this becomes slurred into a mixture of 'above' and indiscriminate 'whhoooing'. But I've always liked it as a notion. Eventually, surely somewhere, somehow, we'll come to our happy abode. Goodness only knows what it'll look like. Maybe we've already been there and didn't recognise it.

I'll take my chances. I'll keep looking. It must be out there.

Keep Right On.

Epilogue
The wide blue yonder

I'LL START with my apologies to Blues supporters.
I am absolutely certain that I will have missed your
favourite anecdote and failed to mention one of your
favourite players. The reason I can be so confident
is that on reading through what I have written I am
astonished at what I have managed to omit. Quite
how I haven't made more mention of Johnny Vincent,
Jimmy Greenhoff, Mark Dennis, Trevor Hockey, Dele
Adebola, Martin Grainger, Olivier Tebily ... and the
list could go on ... is alarming. In my defence, I never
set out to write the full history of Birmingham City
and neither did I claim that I'd cover every great away
day or even each unlikely victory or humiliating defeat.

One of the truly gratifying things about placing
one's thoughts and ideas about anything on public
record is the way in which it provokes genuine,
thoughtful response. Having done so with blogs and
previous publications – not many of them about

football, it's true – I have been genuinely humbled by the trust and effort that has gone into some of the responses I have received. Stories that I have chosen in order to illustrate points or emphasise an observation have often prompted pages of very personal memoirs, recollections and reflections from total strangers. All of which is by way of saying that if you think I've dropped a stupid clanger or been inaccurate in any way, find my details at the end and let me know. If you just want to troll, as some of my respondents choose to do, particularly about my more overtly political stuff, feel free to do so. I hope you'll feel a cleaner, better person afterwards but do let your mum know you've been using her laptop and try to remember to take your dirty dishes back to the kitchen.

Quite what the future looks like for clubs like Birmingham City is unsure, but I am certain of one thing. Reports of the death of the game below the Premier League are hugely exaggerated. The recent woes of established names such as Bury and Bolton have prompted a degree of justified nervousness about what such 'community' clubs will look like in years to come, but this may be too pessimistic. The ascent – even if it turns out to be relatively temporary – of Bournemouth and Burnley should give us cause for optimism. Leicester's astonishing achievement and their current status as a big-hitter has demonstrated that the days when the top four or five places seemed to be predestined by a higher power could be coming to an end. As I write – and I realise that time may bite this observation on the backside – provincial Sheffield United are holding their own in the top flight and our irritating neighbours at Wolves seem to be building something genuinely significant both on and off the field. It was once lazily fashionable to observe that teams climbing up the league and then staying at the top was an impossibility in the modern game. That is demonstrably untrue.

Another cause for optimism is the indestructible affection of the British people for getting out of their houses in all weathers to watch live sport. This applies to many activities other than football, but a glance at the stats is both illuminating and a cause of wonder.

The Championship – the second tier of English football in which we have resided for 36 of the 56 years covered in this book (and don't forget the four years in the third) – still attracts the third highest aggregate attendances in Europe behind the Premier League and Germany's Bundesliga. Over 11 million people go to watch games in the Championship every year as opposed to 13 million in the, admittedly smaller, first level. Stick with the figures for a minute.

32 million people watch football every year in the top four tiers of English football, 25 million in the top two divisions. Nearly half that number, 15.5 million, watch football at levels below the Fourth Division. Think about it. In an age of deadening TV coverage and console-based games, that many people go to watch

football in stadia ranging from former Football League strongholds to corners of recreation grounds with minimalist floodlights and a nan selling teak-coloured tea and sausage rolls. Those sorts of affiliations aren't easily dented.

There is, of course, no escaping the fact that for millions of people, particularly on a global scale, watching football is a television experience. It is a compelling, albeit unwelcome, thought that the crowds of, usually, young people assembled in pubs, bars and cafes around the world to watch big games, decked out in replica shirts and regalia, regard themselves as dedicated a follower of their randomly chosen Premier League giant as I do of Birmingham City. What's more, one way or another, despite my early-bird, pensioner-special, loyalty discount season ticket, they may well put more money into their chosen club's coffers than me. When TV cameras scan the grounds at big league games, it is clear that there are obvious 'tourists' in the crowd, happy to be there, enjoying their selfies and quite probably experiencing one of the main reasons they came to visit the UK in the first place. I can't remember seeing any at St Andrew's, although we found quite a few local day trippers during our Premier League days. If I do ever come across any genuine tourists, I'll be sure to take them aside and explain that an absolute prerequisite for calling yourself a Blues supporter is the stamina and resolve to endure decades of non-achievement with the occasional flirtation with minor success. That should enhance their matchday experience.

Although reminiscence is at the heart of this book, I have tried to keep my initial promise about avoiding nostalgia. On reflection, I'll admit that the line can become blurred. I have tried to write for fellow supporters in a way that has them nodding along remembering their own club's penchant for snatching defeat from victory, along with the long-awaited moments of triumph that really do make it all worthwhile. So, nostalgia or not, I'm going to finish with two anecdotes, both of which are tinged with very personal reflections but which, I hope, speak to you all.

My mother married my stepfather a year after my first foray to St Andrew's. He was a Blues supporter and season-ticket holder. I have no idea whatsoever whether this influenced her choice and I strongly doubt that it did so. It did have the effect of forging something of a bond in what was, as is common in such cases, an occasionally uncomfortable relationship between us. He would often drive me to home games but once parked up, he would set off for the somnolent security of the Main Stand and I would make for the Kop or the Tilton. Circumstances meant, therefore, that we didn't watch games together very often. The last time we did, and it was only shortly before he gave up the ghost on the club and the stadium that had been part of his life, was on 18 February 1984, the day before his 69th birthday.

We were playing West Ham in the fifth round of the FA Cup. At the time, we were hanging around in 18th position in the First Division and West Ham were comfortably in the top half. We were in the heart of the dismal Saunders era. Crowds averaged just above 14,000 over the season. As an interesting aside, the table for the season, in which Liverpool pipped Southampton for the title, reveals that ten clubs in the top flight at that time now, like us, hang around the lower reaches. In some cases, as with poor old Notts County, much, much lower. So a crowd of 29,570, many from East London, plenty of whom were up for something aside from football in those edgier times, was quite something.

My stepfather revelled in the name of Horace – a moniker that even in these trendy times of reviving traditional forenames seems unlikely to make a comeback. Outside his family, he was known more widely as Harry. Around him sat loads of blokes just like himself: old-fashioned, workaday, miserable Brummies. As we chatted amiably prior to the game, one of his companions made the following observation. 'Y'know, Harry, I was just coming up the hill today and it struck me clear as anything.' We waited for the revelation of this thought. 'We ain't got a fucking chance, have we?' We chuckled happily at this unremarkable truth.

In front of the massed West Ham fans in the Railway, we went into a three-goal lead by half-time. As we shook our heads in collective wonder, I turned to pass the time with Harry's companion, expressing the view that his hunch may just have turned out to be wrong. With a straight face and no obvious hint of mockery, he responded. 'Well. I've just done the calculation of how many times four goes into 45. It ain't looking good.' There must be something deeply damaged about our collective psyche for me to admit that I understood exactly what he meant. It was a true nugget of Birmingham City gold.

For the record, we lost in the next round of the cup at home to Watford in front of 40,220 people, and then scraped one win in our final 12 games – at home to the Villa – before being relegated on the last day of the season from a position of relative safety. As referred to earlier, all of this, along with the awfulness surrounding the game in general, became too much for Horace who gave up his season ticket, broke the habit of a lifetime and never went again.

Some years later I went to visit him in the home where he saw out his days fuddled by dementia and physical decay. As usual, he wasn't initially sure of who I was but seemed to be getting there slowly. I had my son with me and I mentioned that we were off to see the Blues in the hope that it would kindle some spark. 'Yes,' he replied. 'We've got Stoke at home.' And we did have. I'm not sure quite what that remarkable tale tells us and I'm not going to imbue it with any sort of pop psychology. But as I approach my own dotage, I'm not sure what it could say about me if I failed to recognise those closest to me while dredging up the fact that we were away at Barnsley (no disrespect intended, Tykes).

Horace had been at Wembley for the 1956 cup final where we lost to Manchester City in a game that has inscribed itself in footballing legend as the one where Bert Trautmann broke his neck and played on, manfully ignoring the nagging stiffness. He'd been through a lot, had the Man City keeper. He had been a prisoner of war and was the victim of much post-war racism and suspicion. He wasn't the kind to allow a severed vertebra to keep him from a cup winners' medal. As we approached our own major Wembley cup final in February 2011, local radio was full of over-sentimental stories of, and dedications to, lost family members who had been there in 1956 and who would be remembered on the day, whatever the result.

Directly next to me on the day of the final was my son, then in his mid-twenties. Around us were, as I explained earlier, people who were known to us as well, of course, as strangers who could yet become subject to random hugging. When the final whistle blew there were plenty of tears around. Not from me. I should, perhaps, have shed a few for Horace and all his like who had endured, like me, decades of non-achievement but who had sidled away without a glimpse of genuine glory. For whatever reason, I was not in that sentimental mode. Not so my offspring, who I noticed was allowing himself a tear or two. We enjoy a close, loving relationship but I didn't ask him then and I have never asked him since what provoked this reaction. I didn't hug him: I left him to savour the moment in his own way. Football lets you do that.

We chase a dream knowing that we may have to settle for less. It's not the worst outlook on life I can think of.

A tableau of mediocrity and very occasional success

My Birmingham-watching career since 1963 in numbers – and why it's always a long season.

Season	Division/tier	Final position
63/64	1	Survived – last day
64/65	1	RELEGATED
65/66	2	10th
66/67	2	10th
67/68	2	4th
68/69	2	7th
69/70	2	18th
70/71	2	9th
71/72	2	PROMOTED – secured on the last day
72/73	1	10th
73/74	1	19th
74/75	1	17th
75/76	1	13th
76/77	1	13th
77/78	1	11th
78/79	1	RELEGATED – confirmed on the last day
79/80	2	PROMOTED – secured on the last day
80/81	1	13th
81/82	1	16th

82/83	1	17th
83/84	1	RELEGATED – confirmed on the last day
84/85	2	PROMOTED
85/86	1	RELEGATED
86/87	2	19th
87/88	2	19th
88/89	2	RELEGATED
89/90	3	7th
90/91	3	12th
91/92	3	PROMOTED
92/93	2	19th
93/94	2	RELEGATED – confirmed on the last day
94/95	3	PROMOTED – secured on the last day
95/96	2	15th
96/97	2	10th
97/98	2	7th
98/99	2	Play-offs
99/2000	2	Play-offs
00/01	2	Play-offs
01/02	2	PROMOTED via play-offs
02/03	1	13th
03/04	1	10th
04/05	1	12th
05/06	1	RELEGATED
06/07	2	PROMOTED
07/08	1	RELEGATED
08/09	2	PROMOTED – secured on the last day
09/10	1	9th
10/11	1	RELEGATED – confirmed on the last day
11/12	2	Play-offs
12/13	2	12th
13/14	2	Survived – last day
14/15	2	10th
15/16	2	10th
16/17	2	Survived – last day
17/18	2	Survived – last day
18/19	2	17th

Index of teams mentioned

L
Leeds United 52, 57, 63, 80, 85, 90, 115–118, 139, 147, 206–207, 213
Leicester City 15, 65–68, 207, 218–219, 242
Leyton Orient 46, 57, 63
Liverpool 15–16, 31, 52–53, 60, 62, 71, 79, 111, 126, 128–130, 135, 138–139, 147, 149, 158–159, 161, 169–170, 195, 208, 223, 246
Luton Town 71, 80, 127

M
Manchester City 52, 121, 248
Manchester United 15, 28, 71, 87, 107, 123, 137, 147, 168, 170, 204, 207
Middlesbrough 71, 115–116, 149–150, 158, 221
Millwall 63–65, 72, 76, 132–134, 144, 154, 192, 206–207, 213, 221
Milton Keynes Dons 182

N
Newcastle United 123, 163, 216
Norwich City 24, 37, 63, 68, 91, 116, 135, 175, 206, 214
Nottingham Forest 15, 60, 120, 185–186, 232
Notts County 30, 97, 246

P
Port Vale 27–28, 77, 204
Portsmouth 109, 159, 169, 177
Preston North End 61–62, 121, 131, 234

R
Rochdale 37, 182–183
AS Roma 203
Romford 107
Rotherham United 37

About the author

Jon Berry is a former teacher, academic and writer who lives in Hertfordshire. He has written widely on education and related matters. In *Boomeranting* he talks about his childhood 'choice' of becoming a Birmingham supporter and of growing up in the city in the 1950s and 60s. His blog at https://radicalreadblog.wordpress. com usually deals with politics, but football features from time to time. You can contact him at nutjon@aol. com – and he promises to respond to your comments, however critical they may be, as long as they are civil.